COWLEY PUBLICATIONS is a ministry of the brothers of the Society of Saint John the Evangelist, a monastic order in the Episcopal Church. Our mission is to provide books and resources for those seeking spiritual and theological formation. COWLEY PUBLICATIONS is committed to developing a new generation of writers and teachers who will encourage people to think and pray in new ways about spirituality, reconciliation, and the future.

A WEEK TO PRAY ABOUT IT

Judy A. Johnson

A WEEK
TO PRAY
ABOUT IT

Cowley Publications
CAMBRIDGE, MASSACHUSETTS

Published in the United States of America by Cowley Publications,
a division of the Society of Saint John the Evangelist. No portion of
this book may be reproduced, stored in or introduced into a retrieval
system, or transmitted, in any form or by any means—including
photocopying—without the prior written permission of Cowley
Publications, except in the case of brief quotations embedded in
critical articles and reviews.

Library of Congress Cataloging-in-Publication Data

Johnson, Judy A., 1951–
     A week to pray about it / Judy A. Johnson.
         p.   cm.
     Includes bibliographical references.
     ISBN-10: 1-56101-246-7   ISBN-13: 978-1-56101-246-6
     (pbk. : alk. paper)
     1. Christian life—Meditations. 2. Johnson, Judy A., 1951–
I. Title.
   BV4501.3.J633   2006
   242—dc22

                                        2005033486

Cover design and photos: Gary Ragaglia
Interior design: Ann Sudmeier

This book was printed in the United States of America on acid-free
paper.

Cowley Publications
4 Brattle Street
Cambridge, Massachusetts 02138
800-225-1534 • www.cowley.org

This book is dedicated to the glory of God, and to all those who have been my teachers—those I've met personally and those I know only through their writings.

Contents

III. Spring

IV. Summer

Pondering:
A Preface

Growing up in a conservative Protestant world, I was taught to disregard Mary, lest I slip into grievous Catholic error. But every year at Christmas, these were the final words the congregation heard from Luke's Gospel: "Mary kept all these things, and pondered them in her heart" (Luke 2:19). Mary put together her ideas and memories: Gabriel's astonishing announcement; her visit to Elizabeth; the journey she and Joseph made to Bethlehem; the coming of shepherds and Magi; and at the Temple, two old people, Simeon and Anna, who had been waiting all their lives to see the baby. She turned these things over and over in her mind and heart, the way a fossil hunter picks up stones in a dry streambed and turns them over, looking for the hidden rune of a life.

Mary pondered events that changed not just her own life but the life of the entire world. These incidents came out of her daily experience as a woman: her pregnancy, her birthing a son, her interactions with both those who came to wish them well and that strong, silent man, Joseph.

I was a shy, introverted child, happiest in books and in the world of make-believe, trying to comprehend events that made no sense: a spine suddenly crooked for no obvious reason; a father who drank; and the discovery that I wasn't, after all, who I'd thought, but had been adopted when I was four days old. I was drawn to anyone else who tried to make sense of confusing events. Despite the anti-Catholicism around me, I forged a secret alliance with this young woman of Scripture.

The ponderings in this volume concern much smaller events than those in Mary's life. As I walk in the woods or enjoy dinner with a friend, the ordinary occurrences that make up the common events of my life, I contemplate their significance. These meditations are the result.

The arrangement of the pieces follows the calendar year and some of the major events in the Church year, starting in autumn. (For those of us oriented to the academic year, September *is* the beginning of the new year.) However, each meditation stands alone; therefore, you can enter the text anywhere and read these in any order.

You are invited to respond to these pieces through the questions for reflection. You may wish to journal your ideas or simply think through the questions. They can also be used as discussion starters in small-group study.

Questions for Reflection

What events in your life do you continue to think over?
What childhood events shaped your life as it is now?

A WEEK TO PRAY ABOUT IT

Spring

Summer

Winter

Autumn

*Season
of Harvest,
Abundance,
and Feasting*

Writers I return to:

Louisa May Alcott
Frederick Buechner
Annie Dillard
Patricia Hampl
Gerard Manley Hopkins
Julian of Norwich
Haven Kimmel
Anne Lamott
C. S. Lewis
Anne Morrow Lindbergh
Kathleen Norris
Chaim Potok
Rainer Maria Rilke
Dorothy Sayers

Classical composers whose music feeds my soul:

Johann Sebastian Bach
  and sons
Aaron Copland
Claude Debussy
David Diamond
George Gershwin
George Frederic Handel
Joseph Haydn
Wolfgang Amadeus Mozart
Giovanni Palestrina
Sergei Rachmaninoff
Maurice Ravel
Nikolay Rimsky-Korsakov
Ralph Vaughn Williams

Artists whose work I must see again and again:

Paul Cézanne
Meinrad Craighead
Imogen Cunningham
Raoul Dufy
Childe Hassam
Claude Monet
Georgia O'Keeffe
Maurice Prendergast
Mark Rothko

A Week to Pray About It

I know I'm in trouble when a priest begins a request with the words, "Now, don't laugh, but" or "Promise me you won't say no until you've prayed about this for a week." That second opener marked my return to teaching Sunday school to teenagers. Adolescents were a group concerning whom I might have said, as my friend Sharon does about other things, "Well, stick me with a fork because I am so *done* with that." Seven years of teaching English in a Christian school, fourteen years of library work in a Christian college—I figured I'd spent enough time helping to raise and educate other people's kids. Teens were squirrelly, opinionated (and so often wrong in those opinions), and potentially obnoxious.

They were also utterly endearing, but I was ignoring that.

A week to pray about something, even if I've already made up my mind about it, gives time for sober reflection. Every day or so, I'd call Kathi, the priest who'd made such a foolish request, with another question.

"Judy, I am so enjoying watching you squirm, because *you* know, as *I* do, that God has called you to this work," she all but gloated during one of our verbal jousts.

Despite my skepticism, I had two inescapable facts before me. On Sunday mornings, watching the acolytes' faces as they walked down the aisle carrying their candles, I had begun going all soft. This part of the service hadn't moved me before; either those particular kids (some of whom would be in my class) were special or something was happening in me.

Some mornings I've coaxed myself to church by thinking about the elderly whom I will see. Marcia, a woman in her eighties, who has for four decades worked with members of our church's Special Class, is my example of faithful service. Once, as I returned to my seat after Eucharist, I noticed an elegant, white-haired woman gently touch the cheek of her newly widowed friend, murmuring simply, "Oh, my dear." I've watched the aptly named Jewell, perfectly coifed and decked out in a lilac suit, inch slowly to the rail with her walker. And so I watch the elders graduate from canes to walkers or wheel-chairs, observing their hands become twisted and mottled with age spots. *You will be there one day,* I tell myself. *See how to do it well.*

We all attend church for a complicated variety of rea-sons, some of them at first seeming to have little to do with worshiping God. Rolling out of bed on Sunday morning gets a little bit easier when I recall those—young, old, or some-where in between—who are connected to my pilgrimage.

Questions for Reflection

If you attend a place of worship or some other group that feeds your spirit, why do you go?

Who are some of the people who have been examples of faithfulness to you?

Dancing Without Chains

"Dancing is just an excuse to put your arms around another man's wife," was a condemnation I recall hearing from the Baptists I knew as a child. Perhaps it's the very prohibition that has made the art form so attractive to me and my two left feet. Not a dancer myself, I will travel a good distance to see a show Twyla Tharp choreographs, even without possessing the language and background to fully understand the performance.

In the Middle Ages, life was sometimes called the Great Dance, as God and all creation—especially the planets and stars—moved together in predictable, orderly, beautiful steps. Sometime after the Enlightenment, we began referring to life in mechanistic, less lovely metaphors.

Yesterday at lunch a friend shared a professor's comment, "You can't dance in those chains." The image struck me. For much of my life, I've been trying to dance in chains heavier than those Jacob Marley wore on his visit to Ebenezer Scrooge. My chains were forged from the requirements of a legalistic brand of Christianity. Was God concerned about whether I wore slacks instead of a dress to work? Was it sinful to watch movies, including children's animated movies? Could it be true that if one didn't have private devotions in the morning, one could scarcely expect to sense God's presence during the day?

Years of struggling to dance in my chains created in me a curious passivity about my life, so that any attempt to change it took on almost mythic dimensions. I acquiesced to the rules, wearing dresses even in the most bitter weather, avoiding all movies, and adjusting my own rhythms to include prayer and Bible reading in the morning. Oh, I understood Sisyphus, laboring up that mountain, pushing a huge rock that was ready to roll back and crush him. Unlike Sisyphus, though, I had times when I felt I couldn't face that rock one more day. Those moments struck even after I'd quit my job and gone to seminary.

During one of those passive days, my friend Sharon Marie was listening to me complain about my post-seminary prospects. From her personal experience of contra dance, she gave me a new way to think about my life through the metaphor of dance. Contra dance is an American folk dance that somewhat resembles square dancing, with callers, set moves, and changes of partners. Sharon Marie told me that one of the worst feelings in the dance is to reach for a partner and not be grasped firmly. Conversely, it is glorious to dance with someone whose clasp offered some weight to rely on when you put out your hand. "Judy," she admonished me gently, "give the Creator some weight."

Thanks to that advice, I've stepped away from the forms of work and religion that put me in chains. I still have my two left feet, but dancing with God and with the people around me has once again become poetic.

Questions for Reflection

What in your life is preventing you from joining the dance?

What steps can you take to remove the chains? Who can help you do so?

How can you give the Creator some weight as you dance together?

A WEEK TO PRAY ABOUT IT

Fresh Out of Answers

I wanted to be a reference librarian, the person with all the answers. On the way to earning my degree in library science, I took specialized classes in reference sources for business and the social sciences. The professor was an older southern gentleman on intimate terms with every book in the library, who delighted in coming up with test questions to stump us. I remember once checking nineteen different sources and still not finding the answer. I hate that.

I did indeed work the reference desk at a college library, making some good and lasting friends in the process. I helped students locate answers to specific research needs and shepherded some of their senior projects. Despite those specialized reference classes, I was a generalist, and I liked that. I could learn a bit about nearly anything in the course of a week.

In my career, no question was too impossible; clear-cut answers were to be found. Life was a true-false test, not a multiple-choice or an essay exam. In my faith life, however, I discovered that Jesus never suggested that entrance to heaven was predicated on passing a theology exam. Jesus said that how we care for the least, the last, and the lost matters more than the fine points of theology (see Matthew 25: 31–46).

A seminary professor told us that although we cannot have certainty, we *can* have conviction. Most things I can't know, being not-God. I wasn't around for the beginning and I won't be around for the end. In between, challenged by the words of Christ, my job is to visit the imprisoned, feed the hungry, house the homeless, care for the sick, welcome the stranger, offer water to the thirsty, and clothe the naked.

I still prefer to be right and hate to admit I'm wrong. I still love to come up with answers, especially in areas such as marriage and child rearing, where no inconvenient experience has yet proven my theories unworkable. But I'm learning to accept the ambiguity that life presents. God knows, and I don't need to.

Questions for Reflection

In what areas of life are you content not to have answers?
How do you live with the questions for which you have no answers?

Mending Nets

Hanging in my office is a copy of an Alfred Stieglitz photograph. In the grainy black and white of the 1894 photograph, a woman wearing a white cap sits at the seashore, needle busy, mending nets. I purchased the treasure sometime during my years at seminary, when I felt that the woman represented the work I was then doing: stitching back together the holes in my life.

Jesus knew about mending nets. Walking along the Sea of Galilee, he'd called the fishermen James and John from mending their nets to mending souls (Matthew 4:21). The nets would have needed regular mending; a good catch could strain the nets to bursting. Routine maintenance, as my mechanics remind me, is key to keeping things moving, a truth that applies to nets, automobiles, bodies, and relationships.

Quite frankly, there are days when all relationships seem to require too much work. As an introvert, I'm tempted to believe I can manage with far fewer of them, to live as I'd decided to do during high school, courtesy of the gospel of Simon and Garfunkel: as a rock, an island, with my books and my poetry to protect me.

As I regard the badly frayed net tangled in my lap, I wonder what threads I can use to mend frazzled or strained relationships. There is an instructive list in the opening verses of the Second Letter of Peter. Beginning with a reminder that Jesus has given us everything we need both for life itself and for godliness, the writer admonishes us to support our faith with goodness, and goodness with knowledge, and knowledge with self-control, and self-control with endurance, and endurance with godliness, and godliness with mutual affection, and mutual affection with love (1:3–8). The list's order strikes me. Mutual affection, so important to me, comes near the end of the list, just before love. Goodness, knowledge, self-control, endurance, and godliness are all prerequisites. These admirable qualities might be the individual threads I can twist together to make a strong cord, as James and John must have done in those days before the invention of the monofilament fishing line that my dad used.

Sometimes our nets break because of abundance; sometimes they're frayed by overuse or lack of maintenance. It matters less how the net was torn and more how we are going to mend it.

Questions for Reflection

What net needs mending in your life?
Where can you begin to repair the threads?

Permission Slips and Mirrors

Linda knew how afraid I was about, well, many things—but especially about my future. (During my first year of seminary, my advisor suggested that I give up terror for Lent. That fit with what I'd read in Psalm 34:4, "I sought the Lord, and he answered me and delivered me out of all my terror." But I hadn't yet experienced that deliverance.) A degree in theological studies didn't seem to lead anywhere except to further school. How was I ever going to support myself and repay my student loans after I graduated?

Although Linda had no answers, she did have a creative solution. Taking her personal blue stationery, she wrote me a permission slip. Two of them, actually. "Judy Johnson has permission . . ." they said, with her signature and date. It felt like having a hall pass for life. Linda's permission slips gave me the freedom to wander in my own life. You'd think that was obvious: who, if not me, was going to live my life? I'd not felt very encouraged to live my life, though. There were so many rules to consider, as well as the opinions, thoughts, and feelings of other people. Quitting my job, changing where and how I worshiped, and going to seminary were all beginning steps, but they were baby steps, and I knew it.

"You will know the truth, and the truth will make you free" (John 8:32). The truth was, I'd always had permission; Jesus said he'd come to offer us an abundant life (John 10:10). I'd listened to too many other voices, however, and lost track of the still, small voice inside that I knew to be God's message to me. Instead of writing, I taught English, worked in a library, edited other people's writing—all of which were honorable and fiscally sound ideas, but not my real task. Linda, along with other new friends, became new mirrors for me, allowing me to see myself differently. They saw someone more competent and more graced than I usually felt myself to be. By reflecting that woman, they encouraged me to become her, to live into the fullness of her.

The *fullmess* of her, I just typed incorrectly. Or did I? Being creative means making a mess, and I'd spent my life in a system that preferred everything—from my desk to my theology—neat and tidy. Linda gave me permission to make a full mess. Having stuck by my own scary dream of freelancing full-time, and having worked through five years of financial struggles to see that choice validated, I've come to rely on the permission I've been given to trust in the wild grace of God and in myself.

Questions for Reflection

What would you do if you thought you had permission?
Who in your life most accurately mirrors your own sense of
*   who you can become?*

One Bread, One Body

"Do this in remembrance of me," the words spoken at the Last Supper, are repeated every week in the liturgy. Remember me, Jesus pleads, as if his disciples were likely to forget him.

And why not? They were consumed, as we are, with the struggle to make a living, to raise a family, to get along in society. Life changes, friends go away—the sea, the boats, and the fishing nets must have seemed to the disciples the only true constants, after the whirlwind they'd entered as Jesus' followers. There were probably plenty of scenes they'd be eager to forget—instances of betrayal, doubt, rebuke, or fear. Hearing that request spoken for the first time, the twelve could not realize the agony the next few hours would bring.

Remember me, Jesus calls across the centuries to us. Trying to remember the name of that yellow flower or when my library books are due, I forget to remember the basics of my faith. I forget to remember Jesus.

Recently I was graced to visit with a beloved professor. As I was leaving his office, he asked me to remember him in my prayers, and then assured me, "You are not forgotten." I was deeply touched by his words—isn't that what we all want, to know that old connections are still important and remembered?

His comment made me think of the Eucharist. I wonder if, in a small way, the sacrament reminds Jesus of us, as well as reminding us of him, the way the rainbow reminded God of the promise not to destroy Earth with a flood. *Ah, yes,* Jesus perhaps says, *there they are, those dear ones, gathered to eat and drink together again. I remember the table fellowship, the rich taste of wine on my tongue. I remember the laughter and good stories, the chunks of bread shared.*

We need to remember our Jesus, a man who enjoyed food and conversation, who chose a common meal as the basis for and sign of our remembering. Which of us has not found lost worlds suddenly, unexpectedly restored in the pungent smell of fried cabbage or the taste of noodles like those Grandma used to make from scratch? Remember, remember. Don't lose your communion with Jesus nor with the others who have gone before and shared in this same heavenly banquet. Remember, and be remembered yourself.

Questions for Reflection

*What repeated events or rituals reconnect you to your
     family, friends, or church?*
*What special memories of meals with others do you
     treasure?*

On the Wind of Praise

In most religions some attempt is made to move the worshipers out of their heads and into their bodies. In the Episcopal Church, for example, we move around during the service: stand up, sit down, kneel, walk forward to kneel, and extend our hands to receive bread and wine. My Buddhist friends ring a bell to signal the beginning or end of meditation, or they walk mindfully in single file, each step an unbalancing and return to balance, human storks elegantly and deliberately moving across the lawn. It's all part of the game—and I mean that in the best sense of the word—we play in religion, trying physical practices that will connect us with the transcendent.

My friend Liz bought a large gong and hung it in a glorious tree near her house along the river. Every time she was grateful, she ran outside and struck the gong. The blue herons didn't seem to mind; perhaps they heard it as a call to worship, too.

A few months ago, I told my Sunday school class of teenagers that we needed tricks to remind us to pray: every time we brush our teeth, perhaps, or put on our shoes, we should give thanks. They looked at me as they often do, with the kindly tolerance one reserves for lunatics. That's all right; I figure if anything I tell them gets through, it will be enough. But I decided to try developing a new habit for prayer myself, adapting Liz's idea of striking the gong.

For my fiftieth birthday, my friends Maggie and Rich gave

me a wind chime. It hangs on the front porch, which is fairly protected from the wind, thus keeping the chimes silent more often than not—a deep pity. Now, whenever I pass the chimes, even if it's just to drop something in the recycling bin, I gently touch them and let them sing the praise that is in my heart. Psalm 121 closes with the promise, "The LORD will keep your going out and your coming in from this time on and forevermore." I am trying to build gratitude into those goings out and comings in, to let the soft clang of music waft on the wind the praise in my heart.

Questions for Reflection

In what ways do you incorporate movement into praising God?

What practices could you use to add praise within the moments of your day?

Thy Name Is Love

This morning I caught myself humming a song that used to make me cry when we sang it during seminary chapels. "Come, O Thou Traveler Unknown" is probably not the best known of Charles Wesley's six thousand hymn lyrics. Composed in 1742, when Wesley was only thirty-five, the poem retells the story from Genesis, chapter 32, of the patriarch Jacob wrestling with an unknown being, possibly an angel. Wesley, in his whopping fourteen verses, conflated that story with the experience of being redeemed by Christ.

We didn't sing all fourteen verses, but chose the ones that gave the outline of the story. In the ninth verse, the speaker Jacob begs of the wrestler, "Tell me if thy name is Love."

The following verse affirms that the mysterious wrestler, often identified as Christ, was indeed named Love. That's usually when I'd begin to cry. I'd lived for so long with a mean, mad God, whose most obvious attributes were his wrath and judgment, that to sing of God as love was always my undoing.

I remember weeping uncontrollably as well on the day in Early Church History class that we learned about Irenaeus, one of the early Church fathers, and his interpretation of the story of Eden. God knew, Irenaeus said, that Adam was but "a little one" in his understanding, and thus prone to make a mistake. That didn't sound like the God of wrath I'd been brought up with, furious with his rebellious creatures who had eaten forbidden fruit. The God Irenaeus described was the God I'd read about in Psalm 103:13, "As a father has compassion for his children, so the LORD has compassion for those who fear him."

Seminary became a means of redeeming the years I'd been force-fed harsh theology. Not everyone needs so radical a solution to correct his or her God concept. For me, though, being immersed in a community of people living out a vision of a God whose name is Love was not so much wrestling match as redemptive melody.

Questions for Reflection

What quality do you most deeply associate with God?
What would be the opposite of that quality, and do you need to consider it as balance for your view of God?

"But What About Me?"

My friend Gary once taught a college student who, when plans were being made that she felt excluded her, would wail plaintively, "But what about *me*?" I think this question could well have been asked by Andrew, Simon Peter's brother, as he is nearly always identified in Scripture. Andrew told Peter that they'd found the Messiah in Jesus (John 1:40–42). Then he all but disappeared from the scene. When Jesus formed an inner circle of three from among the twelve apostles, it was Peter and the sons of Zebedee, James and John, who had been partners with Andrew and Peter in the fishing business they'd walked away from. To all three he gave nicknames: Simon was renamed Peter, the Greek word for *rock*; James and John, known for their quick tempers, were Sons of Thunder. No nickname for Andrew, who as John the Baptizer's disciple, had the wisdom to see Jesus for who he was and then make the introductions. Peter—brash, foot-in-the-mouth Peter, the master of the big gesture, whose lack of subtlety got him into trouble more often than not—would be one of the chosen few.

I wonder what Andrew must have felt when Jesus signaled that James, John, and Peter were to follow him more closely as they trudged up the mountain of the Transfiguration. Did Andrew, seeing the cloud that enveloped Jesus and the three, want to be there, too? Was he jealous of Peter at all? Did he ever get used to not being part of that privileged group? Matthew says Peter and Andrew shared a house; was Peter, who is always named first, the elder brother whom Andrew had hero-worshiped all his life? Only once, in Mark, chapter 13, is Andrew mentioned with the other three, asking Jesus about the world's end.

Andrew was the go-between. He brought Peter to Jesus. He told Jesus about the boy with two fish and five loaves that would feed thousands. Philip came to Andrew with the news that some Greeks wanted to see Jesus, and together the two took the request to Jesus (John 6:8, 9; 12:20–22).

After being listed as one of the disciples in the Acts of the Apostles, Andrew isn't mentioned again, leaving Church history and novelists to fill in the gaps. My favorite story is that Andrew married that excellent housekeeper, Martha. Another tradition says he preached in northern Greece—perhaps invited by the Greeks on whose behalf he'd gone to Jesus?—and southern Russia, crucified probably around 70 CE in Greece. Andrew became the patron saint of both Russia and Scotland.

I'm not the sort of woman around whom a clique of personality, like the one that later centered around Peter, will ever form. I'm quick to have my feelings hurt, to wonder why *her* and not *me*? But there's Andrew, a model of service for me, steadily doing what he does.

Questions for Reflection

With which of the brothers do you identify more, Peter or Andrew?

How can you better focus others' attention on Jesus?

Growing Grandma Genes

I had just about reconciled myself to never having children when a greater horror dawned on me: there would be no grandchildren. However unqualified I felt to undertake motherhood, I just *knew* I would be a splendid grandmother. I wanted to be the oddball and adoring grandmother who also was very wise and took the children on brief trips, opened the world to them, baked them cookies and read them books, and always knew their secrets. And then I could send them home. To be denied both motherhood and grandmotherhood seemed too much of a sacrifice. I had friends who suggested I "adopt" a grandchild from among the offspring of my friends, but the notion didn't seem to help.

My grandmother genes have nevertheless begun to kick in, manifest most generally on Sunday mornings. I can tell that something has shifted internally. I used to complain about the teenage acolytes wearing sneakers and sandals, never dress shoes, and that in *my* day . . . You can see where this was going. Charlotte, my priest and the mother of sons, once explained to me the practical issue of actually getting the kid to *wear* dress shoes, should they be purchased, never mind the other issue of how fast children outgrow the shoes, along with the rest of their clothes. Ah, well, mine was a different age.

I've stopped fuming about it, which is how I know I've crossed some invisible grandma line. The big clunky sneakers have become endearing. The jeans under the acolyte robes are just part of the teen uniform. They are like privileged, adorable puppies, these youngsters, growing into their own versions of what it means to be children of the Church.

This softening is good for me. I still rant to Charlotte about one thing or another; I suspect I'll be an opinionated woman all my life. Still, I'm trying to focus on the dearness of children, their willingness to begin serving as acolytes as soon as they are old enough. Even before that time, they are invited to bring forward the bread and wine for Eucharist, toddling down the aisle proudly bearing a silver salver or glass carafe. They won't share my memories of dressing up for church and Sunday shoes, but they will perhaps think fondly of a place where they were participants in worship, invited fully into the life of the Church before they could tie their sneakers.

Questions for Reflection

In what ways are children welcomed participants in worship or at other gatherings you attend?

How are you part of the lives of OPK: Other People's Kids?

Expecting Expectantly

I love to cook; I hate to do dishes. Because I've lived without a dishwasher for the past seven years, I try to hold these facts in balanced tension, making a meditation of the chore. I light a candle by the sink, put on soothing music, and focus on the pleasant sensation of warm water on my hands. My favorite meditation aid, however, is a card I bought and framed during my first year of seminary. "Expect miracles" it proclaims. Signs of new life—a small blue bird, a cocoon, dogwood blooms, an egg, an acorn—twine among the letters. Sometimes as I wipe the dishes, I name the miracle, the new life I am expecting. Sometimes I wait dumbly for spring in the midst of whatever winter I am experiencing.

As part of my daily spiritual practice, I read the psalm selections appointed in the *Book of Common Prayer*. Each psalm begins with a heading, which is the psalm's first few words in Latin. One day I was struck by the heading of Psalm 40: *Expectans, expectavi.* Although I passed up the chance to take high school Latin, I could see that the words were from the same root word, despite the English translation, "I waited patiently upon the Lord."

Knowing that some languages use repeated words to reinforce a concept, I began to investigate the verse. I discovered that the repeated root word that here was translated "waited patiently," in Hebrew means literally to bind together, perhaps by twisting, and thus to collect. The figurative meaning becomes to expect, to gather together, to look, to tarry, to wait, patiently. Only one other passage in the Hebrew Bible (Psalm 37:7, which uses a different word for *waiting*) employs this construction.

As I try to wait patiently, I can bind together and collect hope. I gather together the gracious doings and people of God, now and in history. I twist together, as if making a grapevine wreath, the memory of Jane Roberts, a woman from my church who loved roses; the hug of a living saint, an eighty-year-old woman who calls me "Baby"; the sound of the river on my morning walk; and the words of the fourteenth-century mystic Julian of Norwich: "All shall be well." I make of all these a living braid of God's goodness, which I can re-collect while I wait for healing and peace.

The first verse of Psalm 40 concludes: "[God] inclined to me and heard my cry." I do not wait alone or without hope. Always the promise remains of new life, light, resurrection: a cocoon, a dogwood flowering.

Questions for Reflection

For what are you waiting?
What examples of God's faithfulness in the past give you encouragement now?

Spring

Summer

Winter

Autumn

*Season of
Resting and
Stillness*

Suggestions for keeping a sabbath:

- avoid anything with a screen: television, computer, film
- refuse to spend money
- bake something from scratch
- meet a friend for a meal or a coffee/tea break
- light candles
- read a holy book or some poetry
- stop multitasking and really listen to music
- stay out of the mall
- walk alone, or with a human or animal friend
- wander a museum or gallery
- visit someone in the hospital or a retirement home

The Christmas Barrel

My mother stored Christmas decorations in a large barrel in a corner of the basement. Shortly after Thanksgiving she would "walk" the barrel up the stairs and into the living room and begin unearthing its contents: both the tawdry and the tasteful.

At some point while helping to unpack the barrel, I would uncover a beloved decoration, perhaps the matching hurricane lamps that I'd forgotten during the course of a busy year. I'd hold the item up and inhale in remembered wonder.

No snob, Mom made little distinction between German glass ornaments and tiny handcrafted pom-pom teddy bears in colors no self-respecting bear would have been seen in. After a certain age, I began quietly rolling my eyes at the kitsch, but she clearly loved the ornaments that friends and family made for her. I considered them undignified; they "cheapened" the look I wanted.

Each year when the tree was completed, Mom pronounced it the prettiest ever, regardless of the number of homemade ornaments hanging on it. Rather than being immaculately designed, my mother's Christmas trees resembled Amish quilts, proclaiming by a deliberate error that God alone created perfect work.

I think that the Christmas barrel may be my new metaphor for this time of year. Much about this holiday season is certainly mere tinsel, none the better for having been available in stores since before Halloween. The traditions and the music are familiar, sometimes lifelong, easily undervalued memories. Occasionally a forgotten treasure emerges. "Ah," I say, dazzled once more by the shimmer of holiday lights in the snow or the majesty of Handel's *Messiah,* "I remember how much I love this."

The Christmas barrel may also serve as a symbol for my own life as I review the year. I'd rather forget about some experiences, just as I'd have preferred a tree without hand-crafted ornaments. However, the trials have something to teach me, some grace to impart as I consider them closely.

Among my Christmas decorations, I now cherish some teddy bear pom-pom ornaments Mom made. I am slowly trying to accept whatever oddities come out of the Christmas barrel of my life, to relax a bit more with all the seemingly incongruous details.

Advent calls us to examine our lives, to reclaim all the incidents—not to dismiss them because they don't appeal to our aesthetic sense. We are asked to seek buried treasure in the everyday holy events. Something special—as common as a stable and as extraordinary as a star—is about to occur. The light we have been steadily losing will shine on us again: the Sun of Righteousness will arise to illuminate our darkness.

Questions for Reflection

How do you integrate the less pleasing elements of your life into the whole?

What special traditions or memories do you associate with the Christmas holidays?

Going Down to Egypt

When I was growing up, I always enjoyed participating in our annual Christmas pageant. Mary had no speaking lines, but neither did Joseph. Actually, Joseph had no direct speeches throughout the entire birth narrative in Matthew. Although we are privy to his thoughts, he never spoke—not to Mary; not to the angel; not to his son, the shepherds, or the Magi. Joseph's role was not to make speeches, but to implement what an angel of the Lord revealed to him in dreams. The commands Joseph received were more than a little odd: to marry a woman carrying a child he knew wasn't his, to protect Mary and the child from harm by going to Egypt, and to return later to Israel.

Through his obedience Joseph incarnated the will of God just as surely as Mary did, although unlike her, he didn't respond verbally. Reading the narrative this year, however, I wanted Joseph to protest: "Egypt! We can't go to Egypt! That's the land of bondage. They used to kill our baby boys there!"

But he said nothing, just headed south with Mary and Jesus. Luke tells us that Mary pondered in her heart the words and events surrounding Jesus' birth. I can't help feeling that Joseph must have been doing some pondering of his own.

The more I considered the surface oddity of Egypt as a place of sanctuary, the more it seemed fitting. Part of Matthew's agenda was to show Jesus as the promised Light of the Gentiles, the fulfillment of Hosea's text, "Out of Egypt I have called my son." (11:1). Beyond that intention, however, the journey to Egypt seems in harmony with other biblical texts. God promises in Joel 2:25, "I will restore to you the years that the locust hath eaten." Did Jesus' presence in Egypt somehow right the ancient imbalance created during the plagues, when locusts devoured the crops?

God redeems not only our present moment but also our past, individually and collectively. We all have our own Egypts, places of unspeakable pain awaiting redemption. Sometimes, however absurd the call seems, we may be asked to revisit those places.

This divine redemptive activity, perhaps symbolized by the flight to Egypt, gives me hope for those times when God asks me to do something that runs counter to my own understanding. It also offers comfort for women, children, and men who have known social and political oppression. It suggests a healing future for a nation still carrying wounds from conflicts more than a century and a half old. It hints at a world that will someday be fully renewed.

Although my traveling plans don't include a trip to Egypt, I've noticed that God rarely consults my itinerary. I choose to believe that sometimes the places of our greatest hardships become the lands of our deepest joys.

Questions for Reflection

What events in your life need to be redeemed?
In what ways do you sense that this redemption may have already begun?

Be Not Afraid

Although the pictographs at the trailhead make it very clear that all dogs are to remain on a leash, the dog owners I meet on the trails can't resist allowing Fido to splash in the river or chase a squirrel. Most of the unleashed are big dogs: Rottweilers and retrievers, shepherds and setters. At another hiker's approach, the owners try frantically to leash their animals again. Because I don't wear a ranger's uniform, I assume they're being kind, thinking that perhaps I'm terrified by their big, slobbering dogs. I always call out, "I'm not afraid!"

Recently I said those words to a tall man trying to grab the collar of his golden retriever. He didn't hear me, but I heard myself. And I knew that I was lying. Although I wasn't afraid of the dog, I was afraid—had been afraid for days about a situation over which I had no control.

As I walked past the dog, I thought about the birth stories in Matthew and Luke. Mary and Joseph might have been afraid of the plans that the angels announced; however, *I* was afraid because the plans I'd made might *not* come to pass. We're very good at planning, we humans, and we do a lot of it—plans and contingency plans, and *what-if*-ing all night long.

I thought about my fear and saw that it was rooted in the old god I used to worship, the one who wanted sacrifice, who might see the ruin of my plans as a worthy offering. Then I recalled God's words to Jeremiah, "Surely I know the plans I have for you . . . plans for your welfare and not for harm, to give you a future with hope" (Jeremiah 29:11).

I need to practice trusting a God who means me well, who comes to me again and again, proclaiming good news that completely scuttles all my carefully made worries and plans. At Christmas we celebrate the God who took on flesh, the God who understands the brokenness of the world we live in, the God who hallows our living and our planning, the God who does not leave us alone. And we learn to trust with Mary, saying, "Let it be with me according to your word" (Luke 1:38).

Questions for Reflection

What are some of your greatest fears?
How have you been helped to persevere despite those fears?

Finding Another Way Home

"You were sealed by the Holy Spirit in Baptism and marked as Christ's own for ever."

"You were sealed . . ."

"You were sealed . . ."

The words of the two women priests overlap as they anoint the streams of people coming forward on this chilly January morning. We are commemorating the baptism of Jesus, and our own baptisms, two long lines of us stretching to the back of the church. The notes of the piano ripple like water behind the priests' soft voices. At coffee hour our foreheads still glisten from the dab of oil. We have been brought together in yet another sacramental act of faith, making the common holy.

We are in the Church season of Epiphany, a word that means "appearance" or "showing forth." At Epiphany we hear about the Magi, astrologers from the East who learn from a star's appearing of Jesus' birth, and travel to worship him. When angels in the shared dreams of these men warned of potential danger from Herod, the Magi had to find an alternate route home.

I would have grumbled about that, I just know it. To go to all that trouble—years of study, really—to be in the right place at the right time to see and interpret the star's appearing. To outfit a caravan, at no small expense, to find a suitably magisterial gift, and to be there in time to see a child—not exactly what we're looking for, but, hey, we can be flexible on this. And then to have to find another way home, through unknown dangers. I'd have wanted my old caravan route back; at least I'd have known what perils to expect.

Jesus comes to shake up the world and my own place in it. Warned neither by angels nor dreams, I'd had only a vague inkling of my need to find another way home. In my mid-thirties everything I'd been taught or experienced had begun falling apart. By God's comic grace, I was first lured into the Episcopal Church by the promise of bagpipers. I knew I'd found an undreamed-of route that first July Sunday. I was employed by a conservative Christian college, however, and to get on this new path would require my resignation. It seemed a lot to ask; I dragged my feet for nearly a decade.

Matthew doesn't emphasize the journey of the Magi. Therefore, we don't know how long they traveled, what route they took, what new way home they found, or how the journey changed them. For me, though, the liturgy and ritual of the Episcopal Church became my new way home, the road I choose to travel in the second half of life and the wellspring of my worship.

Questions for Reflection

What part of your present life isn't working as well as it used to?

Have you sensed a call to find another way?

Pelican Love

It's Lent, not my best time of year, coming as it does in February, my month of remembered sorrows. I've tried to counter my painful memories by writing a list of good things as they occur each day, but retraining the mind and heart isn't the work of a single year or decade.

This week I've been more than usually homesick for people and places that no longer exist as they did forty years ago. I've had dreams about the place I call my home church, the Baptist church whose white pillars supported the front porch and my faith. This morning I wanted to hear that congregation singing again, and in the funny way that grace works, the hymns we sang in church today allowed me to do so.

"My Faith Looks Up to Thee" and "Guide Me, O Thou Great Jehovah" transported me with their familiarity back to my old home church, to a time and a place where as a young person I felt valued. Uplifted and nurtured by those memories, I noticed anew the participation of young people in *our* service: the teen crucifer and acolytes, a teen lector, a teen in the choir, another playing an original piano piece for the offertory, two teens doing double duty as ushers. Some of those teens have been in my Sunday school class; a couple more were sitting a few pews ahead of me, coming after the service ended to hug me. My heart bursts with their beauty and their unspoiled lives.

During the service I glanced up at the appliquéd banner that we display during Lent. A large white pelican on a deep red piece of fabric plucks her own breast, allowing the nourishing drops of blood to fall to the baby pelicans in the nest below her. It's a symbol of Jesus feeding us in the Eucharist, of course. Most weeks I glare at the banner and find fault with the stitching. The fabric puckers in places, something that wouldn't be allowed by my quilting group. Today I look at the bleeding pelican and at the teens around me thinking, *I would do that for these children.* It's what at the best of times all adults do—we bring forth whatever nourishment we carry and offer it to our young.

Questions for Reflection

What memories from your childhood, possibly related to your church experience, do you treasure today?

Are young people active in the organizations to which you belong? How could you make a place for them in your group?

The Imposition of Ashes

I love the ornate language of the Elizabethan age, the words of the Bible I grew up with, of Shakespeare and John Donne, of the *Book of Common Prayer.* I don't even mind the confusion that can result because language changes over the centuries. Wednesday, for example, we are having Holy Eucharist with Imposition of Ashes. It is a solemn service in which we confess all the things that I, for one, would rather forget I'm guilty of: the seven deadly sins and more. Then we are smudged with ashes of the palms from the previous Palm Sunday, which one of the women has carefully burned for this ritual. The priest or liturgist will impose them, making the sign of the cross on our foreheads.

And it *is* an imposition, the mark of those ashes. The powdery ash, liable to sprinkle down on my glasses, forms an awkward cross. Then there's the problem of what to do after the service: Do I leave the ashes in place as a bold testimony of my faith in a world that pays little attention to Lent beyond Shrove Tuesday pancake suppers and sale prices on fish? By leaving the ashes in place, in this pluralistic world, am I imposing my faith on others who don't deserve to have it shoved at them? I have no good answer.

It's an odd feeling, the grittiness of the ashes. The first Ash Wednesday service I ever attended, I was part of the group imposing the ashes. Those of us in the catechumenate, a yearlong preparation for being received into the Church, were to impose ashes, and on Maundy Thursday, we were to wash feet.

I had never done anything like this before, and it frightened to me. What if I did it wrong? As if someone would be judging the symmetry of the crosses I made on the foreheads presented to me!

"Remember that you are dust, and to dust you shall return." It's not too much to ask, once a year. Caesar employed a slave to walk with him and whisper in his ear, "You, too, are mortal." We forget. We dress up in our power togas with the purple band that only Caesars wear, and we forget that we bleed and die.

Today on the altar there were two vases of red and white carnations. They were given to mark what would have been the eleventh birthday of a girl who died just before Christmas in a freak accident with her horse. They stabbed us, those flowers. We are all mortal: those of us affectionately termed "over the hill," even the children, even the still-bright blue jay lying on the sidewalk today.

Questions for Reflection

What signs of your faith do you present to the world?
How do you respond when those not of your faith display
    symbols of their religion?

The Heart of Pain and Ritual

The Charlie Chaplin of cats—dapper, prone to mishap, cheerful through it all—died last November. I knew then for the first time at a visceral level the meaning of the word *inconsolable*. Winter is not a good time for me anyway, and to lose this best-beloved cat, apparently because of bungled care from three veterinarians, was a particularly unexpected blow. I cried every day for weeks, and then my heart went dead and cold. Friends asked when I was getting a new cat; I told them I still had one cat and was enjoying less mess. But I found myself crying for him at odd times, often in church, where I tend to be softer.

After Eucharist one Wednesday morning three months after his death, our assistant rector, Kathi, came and sat down next to me to offer comfort. She said, "I don't have a problem with your still mourning him. I have a problem with the fact that *you* seem to have a problem with it. What about some sort of ritual?"

Ritual is good, I thought. "You think this is somehow your fault, though I don't," Kathi went on. "What if we did the Reconciliation of a Penitent? Then you could feel forgiven."

I decided it might work. Ritual isn't for God, but for us. A ritual is a marker along the journey. So on Ash Wednesday, after being reminded that I too would die one day, I followed Kathi from the chapel to the sanctuary. She told me to sit in the bishop's chair, a massive thing carved of dark wood—it cradled me.

I had never been to confession, though as a child I was surrounded by Catholic family on my mother's side, and so knew something about it. Instead of giving me Hail Marys to say after hearing my confession, Kathi told me to read Psalm 34 daily during Lent as my penance. She chose that psalm, she explained, because it contains the verse that affirms that God is near to the brokenhearted and will save those whose spirits are crushed. "You are brokenhearted," she said, "and you need to know that God is with you." We read it aloud together, sitting there.

There's something inherently lightening about telling my sins to a woman wearing a purple stole, the sign of confidentiality. When I have been tempted to grow angry all over again at the doctors who misdiagnosed my cat's illness, I have reminded myself: "No, you *said* that you forgave them. Move on." I also found comfort in the story of the woman who anointed Jesus' feet with oil. "Leave her alone," Jesus told the accusing Pharisee. "She has done what she could." I had done what I could for my cat, and I needed to leave myself alone.

About a week after the ritual, I called a shelter and chose a new cat. In preparing my present cat for another change, I told her: "It's not that I don't love you or that you are not enough. It's that my heart got bigger." That is at best what both pain and ritual do: they make the heart bigger, allowing us to love more and more deeply.

Questions for Reflection

In what cases has ritual allowed you to move forward?
Are there people or situations you need to forgive and release?

Letting Go of Mistakes

A friend and I were recently discussing our mutual aversion to apologizing. Why should two small words—"I'm sorry"— be so hard to get past the teeth? We are none of us perfect, yet admitting I've made a mistake is never easy for me.

This Lent I'm following a practice suggested in a book I read recently: give away one thing each day of Lent—a smile, a compliment, money, or some tangible object. Living and working in a one-bedroom apartment, albeit one with all the windows anybody could want, means space is always a challenge. So I decided to give away one tangible object every day, adding it to a box I'll take to a local charity. I have strong pack rat tendencies; I figured I could give away one thing a day for more than the forty days of Lent without really being affected by it.

Two weeks into the process, though, I'm about to cross the threshold of what is obvious and easy into what requires some thought. It's the threshold into sacrifice, into giving away something that is truly precious to me simply because someone needs it more than I do. I'm finding it hard to admit my mistakes. All those clothes that no longer fit, clothes I may wear once a year—why is it hard to acknowledge that I wasted money buying them in the first place and pass them on to someone who would use them? Errors in judgment aren't, after all, capital offenses. I tally up the years I've owned a particular garment, hoping that a long investment will make it easier to let it go.

In her later years, Queen Elizabeth I supposedly said that when people reach her age, they take with both hands and give with the little finger. I don't want to be like that. The spirit of Lent—to pray, fast, and give—is the spirit of Christianity compressed and magnified. I wonder what benefits I might gain if I weren't so busy tending my precious things and could learn to hold them lightly and pass them on gladly? Those things also include my need to be right and my many ego needs: to be acknowledged, to be loved at all times, to be perceived as best. If I can begin to open my hands and my heart, allowing God to meet my needs, the approach of old age won't require grasping with both hands.

Questions for Reflection

What are some of the things, physical or otherwise, that you find hard to let go of?

How might you begin to loosen your grasp on these things?

Sourdough Life

I know a man who says he can't sleep if even one dirty dish remains in the sink at night. My friend Lori says her mother couldn't leave for work until every dish was clean and the sink empty. Clean sinks are not among my issues. After a lifetime spent trying to clean up the kitchen—"I don't think I've ever seen your countertop before; it's wood!" a friend commented recently—I have hit upon a new strategy. I deliberately and without guilt leave a dish or utensil in the sink at night, even if I do the dishes after supper. This act is in part because I do not own a dishwasher and because I am a snacker. Beyond those two inescapable facts, however, lies something deeper than just my own brand of neurosis.

People who bake sourdough bread keep a starter batch in the refrigerator. This sacred lump feeds all subsequent loaves they bake. They never use all of the starter, but continue adding to it. When one of the women in my quilting group was offering some of her "starts" of sourdough bread to us, I passed. Keeping sourdough alive seems like more work than I want to take on, especially when others are willing to bake delicious breads. But the glass or dish in the sink at night are my starter dishes. Tomorrow, they say, there will be more food served on more dishes; here's a starter, a preview of coming attractions. They bespeak the abundance of my nourishment, not just in matters culinary, but in all things.

Life comes from life. So I scatter scraps of paper in my office to seed thoughts for writing and I clutter my dining room table with the effluvia of life: bills to pay, magazines to read, reminder notes to buy eggs or a gift bag. I've made peace with my messiness, limiting it to certain areas of the apartment so that I can clear space easily when company drops by. Rather than scourging myself for the precarious piles, as I've done in the past, I tell myself I'm getting better at this housekeeping stuff. Clean surfaces in my own space actually make me nervous, much as I admire them in the homes of friends. Too much cleanliness indicates, for me, that nothing's going on here, nothing's brewing, no alchemy of sourdough leading to a good, solid loaf.

Jesus promised his followers that he'd come to bring them not just life, but more abundant life (John 10:10). God is able to do "exceedingly abundantly above" all that we can ask or even imagine (Ephesians 3:20). God challenged the Jewish people in Psalm 81:10, "Open your mouth wide and I will fill it." I've decided that out of the apparent chaos of my life comes the material for more and more "loaves of sourdough" to be shared.

Three cheers for people who can keep their kitchens clean! But those of us surrounded by clutter can use it to praise God for the richness of our lives.

Questions for Reflection

In what ways does your life express its abundance?
How have you been able to share this abundance with others?

Living Together

The guy who lives upstairs practices tai chi, thumping in the process, just as he apologetically warned me he would when he moved in. The woman who lived next door used to grind fresh coffee beans each morning. What I once referred to as my teacher ears, so valuable when I was in charge of a senior high study hall, have clearly outlived their usefulness. They are maladapted for life in apartments, where walls are usually thin. Some days I long for a house, separate from everyone else, so that I wouldn't know the intimate patterns of my neighbors' lives.

On the other hand, apartment living helps me remember that we are all connected. "We do not live to ourselves, and we do not die to ourselves," as Saint Paul wrote in Romans 14:7, during an extended discussion of being guided by another's weaker conscience. How I live in my apartment affects the quality of life in the adjoining apartments. That was still true on the occasions when a roommate and I were renting a house, but it's easier to remember when I know that a voice raised in anger will travel through the walls.

My mother lived by the code of "What will the neighbors think?" I don't want to be constricted by that question, but I do want to be considerate of others, which is not as easily practiced when living alone. So I take care not to start a load of laundry at eleven at night, even though I could. There's a child living next door now; he needs his sleep, uninterrupted by the whooshing of water from a wall away.

None of us lives to ourselves, even those among us who are single. What we do matters to one another. This was a particularly snowy winter, with heavy drifts in the driveway and school and work cancellations. My neighbors between them own both a pickup truck and a small van. They went up and down the driveway in their vehicles until I could get my little car out, too. I baked oatmeal cookies as a thank-you gift; without their aid I'd have been stuck until the next thaw.

In the Genesis catalog of all that God made, the phrase "and God saw that it was good" serves as a refrain—until the creation of Adam. Then God saw that it was *not* good for the man to dwell alone, even with the animals and the lush garden. Those of us who are single, whether by choice or by difficult circumstances, can take comfort in recalling that we are never alone.

Questions for Reflection

What have you learned from living with other people,
whether in a family, a dorm, an apartment complex,
or a marriage?
What acts of kindness do you and others share?

Believing in the Unlikely

In a dream I had a few months ago, a tiny girl stood on the riverbank, holding her father's hand and staring at the Brooklyn Bridge. With great seriousness she turned to her father, looked up, and announced: "I believe in it, Daddy. I really do."

I keep playing with the image of that intriguing dream. Though I suppose it's been decades since I crossed the Brooklyn Bridge, I like its improbability—its construction, so innovative for its time, and its spider web of lacey steel cables.

The bridge reminds me of the Nicene Creed, which I recite with others at least once a week and which connects me to the communion of faithful Christians around the world and through time. The creed affirms belief in some highly un-likely things, such as the "holy, catholic church" for example. The Church universal has recently experienced major earth tremors. I am forever expecting it to fall down, to collapse or implode. Yet, I am graced to believe in the Church (no matter how often it hurts the world at large and me in particular), to grieve its failures, and to pray for its salvation.

A few months ago, our church's choir sang an arrange-ment of the First Song of Isaiah: "Surely it is God Who saves me; I will trust in him and not be afraid. For the Lord is my stronghold and my sure defense and he has become my salva-tion." I glanced up to see Charlotte, our priest, singing along at the refrain, her seated body swaying to the melody. Both of the chalice bearers and the deacon were also singing quietly as they prepared for Eucharist.

Two of those four people had been integral to my journey to the Episcopal Church seven years earlier. They were part of a delicate bridge that enabled me to walk away from a lifetime of Christian fundamentalism to a Church that loved beauty and word as I do. Constructing that bridge involved many people over many years—a sign for me of the infinite kindness and patience of God. During the song, I thought, as I often do when something touches me during church: *It could all have turned out so differently, but here I am. What a miracle!*

I need to be reminded of all the bridge connections that God has woven into my life: lovely musical settings of Scripture, the fragrance of peonies, or a line of turtles sunning on a fallen sycamore in the river. These gifts also form tendrils to support my apparently fanciful yet steel-strong belief. The little girl in my dream could see the bridge, and therefore believe, no matter how unlikely that bridge appeared.

Questions for Reflection

What sustains your faith in God or in the Church?
*How do you reconcile the problems of the Church with the
    great blessings it provides?*

Let No One Despise You

Imagine yourself as a young priest or pastor, fresh out of seminary, miles and miles from anything and anyone you've ever known, at your first church appointment. It's not quite what you'd expected. For one thing, many of the people in your congregation—people the age of your parents and grandparents mostly—are more likely to pat you on the head than listen to your carefully crafted sermons. They certainly don't come to you for counsel. You feel the way you did when you were on the edge of puberty, waiting for something to change so you'll look like the adult you know you are.

And then you get a letter from your mentor, the man who got you into this mess in the first place. He writes, "Let no one despise your youth, but set the believers an example in speech and conduct, in love, in faith, in purity" (1 Timothy 4:12).

We memorized that verse as teenagers in my church, we who were among the first to identify a generation gap. We may as well have been carrying banners with the emblem used by a colonial Marine corps from Philadelphia: a coiled snake with the motto "Don't tread on me." But now, in the second half of life, those words of advice to Timothy have taken on a new meaning for me. You already know that the young people in my church are the most gifted and dear teens walking. I'm not likely to despise them. But I've sensed for a long time a kind of reverse ageism in my thinking. "Haven't hit your midlife crisis yet? Please." The girl who was once warned not to trust anyone over thirty is now a woman prone to roll her eyes at those immature people under fifty. I catch myself, and instead remember the words of a pastor who, when I was a child, referred to me as "my little sister in Christ." These still-so-young forty-somethings are my little brothers and little sisters in Christ.

The truth is that we're all too ready to group people into *us* and *them* in so many categories: age, religion, gender, race, sexuality, politics, income, education. It's easier to divide into little camps and protect our fiefdoms than to find common ground and begin to talk to one another across whatever great divide we have created. We don't so much celebrate diversity as we magnify difference—and then distrust it. I know this because I know my own heart—its biases, prejudices, and preferences.

Let no one despise you, a wise mentor counsels. Don't give others any grounds to despise you. By your example of virtue, show what is most lovely in the faith tradition you are trying to live out.

Questions for Reflection

What throw-away remarks do you find yourself making about people who are older or younger than you?
How might you bring together for conversation people of different ages in your faith community?

Come Forth!

One of the joys of attending the seminary that I did was the cordial relationship among a consortium of theological schools in the area. I could drive ten miles and enter a completely different world, a seminary where only men were preparing for the Catholic priesthood. I adored their library. Not only did it contain more of the resources I needed for medieval studies, but it also displayed art objects I loved: a smooth, gray stone carving that sat on the circulation desk; a bowl and chopsticks upstairs on a table; and a statue of Moses, the two tablets held above his head, a second before he hurled them to the ground in grief and rage.

I was most drawn to a statue of Lazarus, and always stopped to visit. The first time I saw the statue, which depicts the story from John's Gospel, chapter 11, he took my breath away. Mary and Martha send word to Jesus that their brother Lazarus is ill, but Jesus sits around for a few days before heading to his friends' home in Bethany. Lazarus has been dead and buried four days by the time the tardy Jesus shows up, and both sisters say the same thing: "If you had been here, my brother would not have died."

Even though Jesus knows exactly what he is going to do (had in fact explained it in a veiled sort of way to his disciples), when he arrives, he cries for his friend. Then he goes to the tomb and has the mourners roll away the stone, despite Martha's practical protest: He's been dead four days and he stinks.

Using a voice to wake the dead, Jesus calls, "Lazarus, come forth!" (When I was growing up, someone said that Jesus had to mention Lazarus by name; otherwise, every dead body in the place would have responded.) And out hops the man who had died—hops, because he's still bound hand and foot.

The statue I love is terra cotta, with a textured white wash over parts of it for the linen wrappings. Lazarus is sitting up, the linen wrapping over his face slipping just enough so that we can see he's startled to hear his friend's voice. His knees are bent and he's resting his weight on his hands, about to try to stand.

That statue felt like an accurate representation of my life during seminary. So many hopes and dreams dead, stinking with rot, myself bound for a long time—and then I heard him call my name.

Questions for Reflection

What part of your life feels as if it's dead right now?
How would a resurrection of that part of your life make you feel?

Longing for Spring

I am old enough to remember the tin box that sat on our front porch, mysteriously visited by a never-seen milkman before I woke up each morning. In that box he left cream, glass bottles of milk, or bright metal containers of cottage cheese. We had a bread man, too, whose white van doors opened to reveal boxes filled with the most luscious chocolate layer cakes ever consumed, never mind the bland white loaves of bread.

In the midst of one of the times when Jerusalem was suffering destruction at the hands of her enemies, one writer likened God's mercies to that daily, mysterious delivery: they were new and fresh every morning. Saying those words makes no sense as you watch the city you love burn. But the Hebrew Bible book called Lamentations, traditionally held to be the work of Jeremiah, proclaims, "The steadfast love of the Lord never ceases, his mercies never come to an end: they are new every morning; great is your faithfulness" (3:22–23). Near the middle of five chapters filled with anguish, this verse is a hope-filled pivot. Before it and after it, the writer is mourning.

A long, hard winter is ending. Yesterday my soul friend and I spoke of the deep longing for spring—crocuses in her yard were blooming, a very delicate shade of yellow and a patch of purple. When every morning dawned gray and the sky was nothing but heavy snow clouds just waiting to unload, spring seemed an impossible fantasy; but now the birds have returned and small green shoots have pushed up from Earth. Life is like a bread truck, like the milkman. Every morning there's something new and fresh delivered to my door: the jay that just flitted across the window out of which I've been staring, wondering how to write about life's daily grace, or the prospect of dinner with a friend tonight. And there: this season's first fly, a miracle of iridescent wings and annoyance. It's easier for me to see the miracles when the sun's out and the sky is a clear blue, with five baby raccoons tumbling over the old wooden chair in the front yard and work before me. And on those gray winter days, there's longing, which I know is most deeply a longing for the God who is described as Light.

The Book of Lamentations ends badly. The last verse seems to offer no hope: "unless you have utterly rejected us, and are angry with us beyond measure." In 586 BCE, there didn't seem to be much about which a writer could be hopeful. The Babylonian armies of Nebuchadnezzar were overrunning the land, and people were being slaughtered or dragged off to Babylon in chains. Yet the people would return and rebuild, that hope of besieged people everywhere, of today's refugees from Bosnia and Rwanda: return and rebuild. Whatever life hands us, there is the longing for light and for spring, for new beginnings and promised mercies delivered fresh to our door every day.

Questions for Reflection

What are some of the mercies in your life?
What steps can you take to remember these mercies on
  dark days?

*Season
of New
Beginnings*

 Spring  Summer

 Winter  Autumn

Some flowerings in my neighborhood:

snowdrop	Bradford pear
crocus	daffodil
Dutchman's breeches	tulip
forsythia	viburnum
redbud	dogwood
flowering cherry	flowering quince
paperwhite	jack-in-the-pulpit
trillium	wood violet
Virginia bluebell	iris
magnolia	bridal veil

Firebird

Growing up a Baptist, to me Lent meant only that some of my classmates gave up chocolate. That renunciation alone was enough to make me happy not to observe Lent. As I got older, however, I began to feel that our Easter celebrations lacked something: we didn't plod through Lent, didn't agonize through Holy Week. I can't say that I now enjoy Lent, but I do see its necessity.

At my church on the last week of Epiphany, we arrive to find printed *Alleluia*s placed in the pews. As the service ends, we somberly place these in a wooden chest, its appearance reminiscent of pirates' chests used to bury treasure. The symbolism holds; we bury the alleluias for Lent. The wooden chest sits at the base of the altar until Easter, when the words, tied to balloons that decorate the sanctuary, greet us as we enter.

The movement from heaviness and solemnity to joy is often expressed in music, even in works not written overtly for the Easter season. A few years ago during the first week of Lent, I sat in Dayton's new performing arts center listening to a program that included Igor Stravinsky's *Firebird Suite.* I found myself unexpectedly moved.

When I listen to the piece at home, I have the same response. It's hard for me to breathe as the music builds to a climax, even though I know how the music and the story end. I weep every time I hear it. Presbyterian minister and writer Frederick Buechner suggests we should pay attention to our tears, especially the ones that surprise us. So I continue thinking about those tears.

The *Firebird* is based on a Russian folktale about a green-taloned ogre who steals the thirteen princesses of light, plunging the land into darkness and despair. A prince has captured but released the firebird. In gratitude for its life, the firebird gives the prince one of its magic feathers. With the help of this powerful talisman, the prince rescues the princesses and kills the evil one.

As I listened to the suite's final movement, I imagined I heard footsteps slowly headed toward Golgotha, followed by the Great Victory, celebrated with drums banging and cymbals and triangle joyously, madly clanging. Yes, I thought, it's Easter, all out of liturgical time.

The Easter story is told in so many ways, by many cultures, over and over. Tears and darkness and death are not the last word. The stories all say that Something or Someone noble—call it a Firebird, a Phoenix, a Christ—is behind every created thing, and that this noble being has somehow conquered all that breaks our hearts. Alleluia!

Questions for Reflection

What pieces of music or art especially move you?
What unexpected tears have you experienced that you need to consider?

Being Kneaded

This is Maundy Thursday, the day on which we commemorate the meal at which Jesus told his disciples, "A new commandment I give you, that you love one another." I used to think that *maundy* was verbally related to *maudlin,* which is how I feel after the service. Actually, it's connected to *mandate,* and thus to the word *com-mand-ment,* just in case you wondered. At my church we will share a simple meal, breaking bread together before walking with candles down a dark hall and up the stairs to the sanctuary, singing as we go. Then we will watch the women of the altar guild strip the altar and remove all traces of decoration from the church.

Anticipating this ritual, I am in my kitchen completing the first step of baking the bread for our meal together. Over this bread Charlotte will say special words, and it will become the body of Christ. Kneading the wheat flour mass, I feel a kinship with Mary. I, too, am making Jesus, though externally, not needing an obvious intervention of the Godhead. Just common bread, kneaded and then set to rise in a warm place.

As I sink into the rhythm of kneading, I also feel united to those women who prepared the Passover feast Jesus ate on his final night with the disciples, although they probably used coarser grains and stone kneading boards. I am also one with nuns and monks down through the ages, baking bread as a gesture of hospitality or for their own needs or to sell. It's the simplest thing, bread, but it connects me with the communion of saints, with all those hungry for nourishment, and with women in developing nations who fetched water this morning to make plain, flat breads for themselves and their families.

Making bread requires the common stuff of life—salt, flour, water. So, too, God takes the common events of our lives to shape and knead each of us into a nourishing loaf. We are broken by life events, and then enabled to share with others whatever grace and comfort we have been given.

Questions for Reflection

What common things in your life has God used to shape you? How are you sharing with others the good things God has given you?

On the Way to Forgiveness

I said I'd forgiven him, but I hadn't. He was one of three veterinarians—of the five we eventually saw—whom I held culpable for my cat Jeb's death. They had misdiagnosed, been careless, ignored my intuition; they had failed to help, and in my book, medical people aren't allowed fallibility. I wrote angry letters to those three after Jeb died, and I swore I would never again set foot in that clinic.

Never is one of those words that should be uttered only in contexts such as "Never allow a child to play with matches." Not quite six months after Jeb's death and about a month after I had ritually affirmed my forgiveness of those all-too-human veterinarians, a friend's cat needed to be put to sleep. Finally facing that reality, my friend called me one morning and asked me to go with her to have her pet put down. Guess which clinic I drove to and which vet walked into the examining room?

He didn't connect me to the events of half a year before or to the blaming letter. He saw many animals and owners each day, and I'd let my hair grow. He focused on the sick cat and her owner, giving me a chance to study him.

Until his grievous failure with Jeb, I'd always liked him. Now as I watched him carefully examine the cat before him, I saw that his sandy hair was thinning and going gray. There were flecks of gray in his beard, too. We all age and grow feeble and die. The cat on the table was fourteen, sick and weak, though still yowling his protest at being taken to the vet. The professional, the crying women, the thin Siamese: we were all mortal, and there was no help for it. We do the best we can. And sometimes we fail. We can't eliminate pain or suffering despite our technology, our maps of human and cat genomes. Life and death is not our call.

This vet was very tender with the cat and with my friend. He didn't want to rush the decision, was honest about what it would take to get a three-and-a-half-pound cat back to some quality of life, if that were even possible. After the injection, he offered to carry the cat back to the car, helped my weeping friend put her beloved pet into the carrier, told her she could settle the bill later, and let us leave by the back door. My heart cracked open for all of us, just doing the best we could. I made it a little bit further on the way to fully and truly forgiving this man and his colleagues. It was Good Friday.

Questions for Reflection

In what circumstances do you find forgiveness difficult?
How do you—or how might you—work through those
  difficulties?

Harrowing Hell

The man standing on the single-plank bridge stretches out his hand to those below him, huddled in a cave. They in turn reach for his hand, which I now see bears the mark of a nail in the palm. I'm looking at an icon known as the harrowing of hell, one of my favorite segments of the Christ story.

Maundy Thursday, Good Friday, Holy Saturday—the great three days, or Triduum, are the linchpins in the world's redemption. On Holy Saturday, a quite dead Jesus goes to hell, the place where all the dead are, because heaven has not yet been opened. There, according to 1 Peter 3:18–19, Jesus preaches to the spirits "in prison," who never had a chance to hear the Good News. He then harrows hell while standing on his cross, which has become a bridge of safety, reaching down to the righteous dead—Adam and Eve, David, and other familiar figures from the Hebrew Bible.

He *harrows* hell. The Old English word from which the verb comes means "to pillage or plunder." According to the imagery of early Christian theology, the triumphant Christ raids Satan's domain and takes the souls whom he has redeemed, the way any conquerer takes the best of a defeated enemy.

Granted, I have some problems with parts of this interpretation of God's redeeming activity. Jesus as Genghis Khan or Attila the Hun doesn't sit well in my mind. But I can broaden the interpretation: more than once, Jesus has brought me out of a hellish situation or state of mind.

On the night of his arrest, as Jesus shared a final meal with his followers, he told them to do for one another what he had done for them. Although he was speaking literally of washing feet as a sign of humble service, all of Jesus' life was meant as an example. In a sermon, Peter described Jesus as one who went about doing good (Acts 10:38). Whenever we do good for one another, we're imitating Christ.

Each of us has opportunities to reach back and pull a companion from his or her personal place of torment. I think, for example, of so many people who were kind to me when my mother died. Gary drove me nearly four hundred miles to and from Akron to say good-bye to my mother. Alicia gave up three days of her summer to take me back there for the funeral. Joe arranged for the reception at his church after the graveside service. Lori called daily and sent a stuffed bear to whom I could confide my grief. When we are strong, we can help others bear their trials. And when we are in hell, we reach up to grasp the hand of a friend.

Questions for Reflection

In what hellish situations have friends or family given you a hand?

How have you helped others who are in difficulties?

Seeing with Opened Eyes

Open our eyes to see your hand at work in the world about us, the priest prays during the Eucharistic service. That plea for open eyes reminds me of one of the great stories from the Hebrew Bible. During their war with Israel, the Syrians find that their battle plans always seem to be known in advance. When the Syrian commander, Ben-hadad, asked who the mole could be, one soldier fingers the Israelite prophet Elisha, who can somehow predict accurately any moves the Syrians intend to make. Ben-hadad logically decides to besiege the city where Elisha is staying. Seeing the army, the prophet's servant becomes alarmed. Yet Elisha tells the young man not to worry, and prays, "Open his eyes that he may see." Sure enough, the young man then sees that the mountain is filled with horses and chariots of fire around Elisha.

In a nice twist within the story, God strikes the Syrians with temporary blindness. Pretending to be helpful, Elisha leads the blinded army right into the midst of their enemy's capital, where Elisha then repeats his prayer for eyes to be opened. He tells the Israelite king not to harm the Syrians, but instead to give them bread and water before letting them go—a generous way to treat one's enemies! "So the bands of Syrians came no more into the land of Israel," the text says, demonstrating a practical outcome of loving one's enemies. (See 2 Kings 6:8–23.)

Although I've never been a patient person, on a recent grace-filled day, the delay at the drive-through bank window was just fine. I settled in to wait and, with nothing in the car to read, checked out the view.

I'd already read the FDIC notices posted on the bank window to my left, so I looked instead to the right—and beheld a miracle. Still bare in the March chill, a midsized tree stood, hung with suet and seed feeders. A couple of redheaded woodpeckers and some chickadees were noshing. Underneath the tree, pecking away at the crumbs that remained, were sparrows, perhaps, or wrens.

From the state of the suet cakes, it was clear that this bounty hadn't arrived that day. How many times, I wondered, had I been preoccupied with my own financial details, never noticing the well-attended bird banquet some thoughtful bank employees had prepared?

Open our eyes so that delays aren't irritations and seeming catastrophes do not unduly alarm us. Open our eyes to notice the angels shimmering all around us in the morning sun.

Questions for Reflection

How do you deal with the frustrations of delays?
What practical use might you make of the time you spend in traffic jams or waiting in store lines?

Foot and Hand, Eye and Ear

Last year was a particularly tough one for the teens of my village. In April, that famously cruel month, just short of her eighteenth birthday, a popular graduating senior was killed in an automobile accident.

It's April again. The other day I drove past the high school as I left the village. There's a big rock on the school's front yard, generally announcing fund-raising events or encouragement to a sports team. This week the rock's been drenched in purple paint, with the young woman's name and a flower painted on it. Below the rock, students have been leaving tributes to commemorate this first anniversary of her death.

I love my village for any number of reasons, among them its recognition of the need for all of us to nurture young people. We have a skateboard park and a center where teens can hang out. After some recent troubling events, the village held public discussions about how to help. The school systems are known for excellence and creativity.

This village of four thousand souls nurtures all its residents in other ways as well. We joke about our unusually high number of massage therapists, yoga instructors, and alternative healers per capita. Several bookstores, art galleries, and an art theatre, as well as fine dining and live music venues, offer opportunities to feed the spirit. This is home to a liberal arts college that hosts peace conferences and writing conferences. The phone book lists fifteen religious organizations and churches. Every summer, the Kids' Playhouse performs. And a forest and river of great beauty border the village.

I live here by the grace of God and my friend Sharon Marie, who found my apartment for me while I was still in shock over being finally done with school (on either side of the desk) at forty-five. The village has nurtured me in the way I have preferred: benignly letting me be. This is a fine place to find the quiet and solitude I need to create. When I am too much alone, I can wander downtown, stopping at the library or the deli or the florist's. People in these places smile and occasionally make conversation, allowing me to sense a connection without feeling overwhelmed.

It takes a village to raise a child and to mourn her, and to raise an adult, too. Saint Paul reminds us that the foot and the hand are connected, the eye and the ear must work together. No part of the body can say it has no need of the other. Furthermore, he continues, the less attractive parts of our bodies receive greater care and protection (1 Corinthians 12:14–26). Most of us harbor some painful memories of being teenagers; it's at best an awkward time. All the more reason for giving extra attention to the young people around us. Child, adolescent, or grown-up, living in a village or a metropolis, we all suffer and rejoice together.

Questions for Reflection

*How does the place where you live nurture you? What about
   it makes you proud?*
*What steps might you take to make that place more inviting
   to young people?*

Late Bloomers

Outside, in other people's yards, purple crocus and white Dutchman's breeches brighten these last winter days. My own bulbs, in a too-shady spot, are far behind, mere green shoots. So in my kitchen I am encouraging some paperwhites in a blue bowl—*encouraging* them, not *forcing* them. I don't suppose bulbs like being forced to do something any more than I do. So I give them little sips of water and place them in the windowsill, trying to keep Monica-cat from nibbling what has begun springing up.

"We all unfurl at our own pace," my friend Liz said the other day, and *unfurl* is just the right word, because it's a leaf here and a bloom there until the flower is revealed.

We were speaking about late bloomers, which is what I've always considered myself to be. I told her my discovery that sycamores, the trees that encourage me all winter with their stark white trunks, are among the last to leaf in the spring. They make up for their tardiness with their dinner-plate-sized leaves and exquisitely beautiful bark.

I like the idea of unfurling, one leaf at a time. Despite the flowering spring bulbs and my delight at the return of color to the gray world, autumn is my season. Only at midlife have I felt at home in the world, in my body, in the Church. I consider myself a chrysanthemum; I'm beginning to enjoy what I hope will be the many-petaled bloom of that flower, unfurling one petal at a time. I've felt pinched back during my summer years, when I was trying to bloom before the season was right.

I recognize that autumn sets limits; a touch of frost in the air makes the blooming more dangerous. "To everything there is a season," the writer of Ecclesiastes says. When spring's bright tulips and iris have gone to seed, and summer's roses and peonies are only memories, it's time for the chrysanthemums and asters among us to blossom.

Questions for Reflection

What season would you choose to describe your life and blooming?
What blossoms are you unfurling?

Consider the Wild Violets

In the Sermon on the Mount, Jesus offered his followers what in some Bibles is subtitled *The cure of anxiety: trust in the Father's care.* This heavenly care extends to all the familiar items of daily worry-currency: food, clothes, appearance. "And why do you worry about clothing?" Jesus asks the would-be fashion mavens among us. "Consider the lilies of the field, how they grow; they neither toil nor spin, yet I tell you, even Solomon in all his glory was not clothed like one of these" (Matthew 6:28–29).

When considering the lilies, don't picture those hothouse lilies standing so proudly in their foiled and beribboned pots around the altar on Easter Sunday morning. The lilies Jesus talked about were wildflowers (perhaps, scholars think, delicately swaying golden anemones) in the Galilean countryside: abundant, colorful, and not long lasting. He called them the clothing that the grass wears.

After receiving three times the usual amount of rain this year, California's Death Valley has burst into bloom, just as the Scripture promises: "the desert shall rejoice, and blossom as the rose" (Isaiah 35:1). This colorful spectacle of Desert Gold, Gravel Ghost, and Desert Five Spot cloaking Death Valley National Park occurs only at decades-long intervals, because the wildflowers can't tolerate the usually intense temperatures.

Here in more moderate Ohio, we've had a rainy spring, too. Everything is verdant; bluebells adorn the park. Yesterday

I was enchanted by a friend's yard, where not only dandelions but also wild violets were everywhere. (She'd like you to know that she really tries to keep her yard mowed, but it's just been too wet.) There's abundance in the wild violets, not only growing in her yard but also sprouting from apparently dead stumps in the glen.

Despite having for many years loved these words from the Sermon on the Mount, I can worry as well as anyone, mostly over things I can't control or that don't really much matter in the big picture. The old saying is true: "Worry is like a rocking chair; it keeps you busy but doesn't get you anywhere." To stop the useless movement of that metaphorical rocking chair, I head for the woods. The wildflowers there offer a visible bouquet of God's loving care for the big and small matters of my life.

Questions for Reflection

About what things do you find yourself worrying?
How might you begin allowing God to take care of them
  for you?

Going Down to Go Up

The proof that I'm not in as good a shape as I was last fall, after I'd spent months walking regularly, came yesterday: I spent a lot of time huffing and puffing as I walked in the glen nearby. More than a hundred stone stairs go down from and—more painfully—back up to the parking lot. Yet after a friend commented the other day on the beauty of the trillium, I had to risk those steps. The trillium were indeed scattered on the hills like stars in the sky, the creek was running merrily, and the water I'm not supposed to drink from the springs tasted fine.

The literal paths in the area, which includes a glacier-carved gorge, offer apt metaphors for life. Go down to go up. That's the point of Jesus' parable about choosing a seat at a banquet where all guests are arranged by rank. If name tags aren't provided at the place settings, choose the lowest place, Jesus cunningly says, so that your host may move you to a more honored place at the table—a far more preferable scenario than being told to step down. Those "who exalt themselves will be humbled," Jesus concludes, "and those who humble themselves will be exalted" (Luke 14:7–11). It's what my priest calls the upside-down, inside-out world of the Gospel.

Most of my walks aren't terribly strenuous. I tend to prefer walking beside still waters and on a level path (Psalm 23:2, 27:11). But of course those stairs are good for me—good for my heart, good for my calf muscles. The path often calls out with enticements of spring wildflowers or spring water, the lure of a blue heron or deer feeding quietly in the morning peace. So beckoned, I choose my path, sometimes going down to go up.

Questions for Reflection

If you had to describe your daily walk of life, what image would you use?

What steps might you take to strengthen your heart physically or spiritually?

Running Away from Home

Late yesterday afternoon I ran away from home. You'd think that living alone, I wouldn't need to pack my little red Radio Flyer wagon and trot off, but it isn't so.

My computer had eaten the whole day's portion of the document due to my employer in a few days. Hours of words had vanished, and though I made a frantic phone call to a technician, there was no help for it. The literal work of my hands was gone.

I tried to tell myself it wasn't so bad. After all, I hadn't lost my ideas or my sources, merely time and effort. I wasn't at the hospital or waiting for test results, nor in danger nor hungry nor cold. I was just mind-weary and frustrated. None of that pep talk helped.

Seeking comfort, I went to that other church, the bookstore.

A prominent theologian-author was presenting ideas from his new book. I'd already planned to attend, although I'd not expected to go feeling as if I were fleeing from something. During the drive I began breathing deeply again. Then I noticed the white blossoms of the Bradford pear trees against the sapphire sky. By the time I sat down in the back of the reading area, I was beginning to feel better.

The man spoke about Jesus for an hour. I took two pages of notes, eager to share what I was hearing with friends. When I left, the sky was the color of peaches, and the Bradford pear blooms looked softer. I stood outside for a moment to admire the view. Then I wandered into an upscale grocery, looking at the rich colors of organic produce—eggplant, yellow peppers, broccoli—and at cheeses, such as L'ossau-iraty and Castergnica, whose names I couldn't pronounce. I bought myself some flowers.

As I drove home, I began really listening to the tune I was humming. It was a song from my childhood, I realized, one that combines a simple chorus and a sweet melody.

> *Turn your eyes upon Jesus,*
> *look full in his wonderful face,*
> *and the things of Earth will grow strangely dim*
> *in the light of his glory and grace.*

My computer isn't better yet; it's going back to the shop on Monday for a tune-up. I still had to spend hours re-creating the work I'd lost, rather than moving on to the next chapter as I'd planned. Nothing changed—except me. This morning I read that God is the restorer of my soul and the helper of my countenance (Psalms 30 and 42). A grace-filled hour among like-minded people, listening to someone tell me about Jesus, allowed me to come back home.

Questions for Reflection

What circumstances make you want to run away from your life?

What measures have you tried or might you take to help you remain at home?

The Fragrance of Life

To those contentious Corinthians, Saint Paul wrote, "But thanks be to God, who . . . through us spreads in every place the fragrance that comes from knowing him. For we are the aroma of Christ to God among those who are being saved and among those who are perishing" (2 Corinthians 2:14–15).

Each of us wafts not only that distinctive scent arising from our bodies and any fragrances we wear, but also the scent of Christ. It's not meant to be overpowering, but attractive. It's more like those old cartoons showing a cherry pie cooling on a windowsill, its delicious odor shaped like an outstretched arm and a crooked finger traveling to tickle the nose of a napping person, luring him or her to the pie.

My mother in her later years became a compound scent of Noxzema skin cream and Hall's cherry cough drops, replacing the aroma of nicotine, sugar from the candy factory where she worked, and the Avon perfumes she loved. She died in the month of July. In September friends helped me move some of her promised furniture to my own home. The house sold in December; I walked around the empty dwelling in March for a final time. In none of those months had I thought about her flowers, beyond regretting that I couldn't transplant the climbing red rosebush that grew by the garage.

In all the wintery details of settling the estate, I'd forgotten that a sweet scent surprised and delighted anyone approaching the front steps of her house during Ohio's late springs.

Invisible, hidden under the rhododendron, lily of the valley bloomed.

When my friend Alicia at last asked, "Did you bring back any of the lily of the valley?" I was stricken—shouldn't I have thought about them, brought something *living* from my mother's home as a reminder of her? "Never mind," Alicia said. "I'll give you some of mine."

Those lilies survived and spread. Tonight, after a walk spent admiring the forsythia and magnolia in bloom around the village, I came home and scraped wet clumps of oak leaves from a small bed along the driveway. As I'd suspected, the small bright green shoots were making their first appearance. In a few weeks, they will open in time for Mother's Day. They will remind me of my mother and of the need to be a fragrance that gives life.

Questions for Reflection

What scents do you associate with childhood memories?
What qualities do you think make a Christian attractive to
others, as a pleasant fragrance attracts?

On the Death of Tulips

A thousand World War II veterans are dying each day now. Yesterday I attended the funeral of one of those veterans.

I'd known Wayne for only the last few years, and then mainly by association. He was the husband of Mae, one of the women with whom I quilt at church on Wednesday mornings. He'd read in another room while we worked, joining us at ten o'clock for Eucharist. Sometimes, when we shared the peace during that service, he called me Carol—not that he wasn't sharp in every way, just that I somehow reminded him of his daughter, Carol. It was a huge compliment.

I discovered that I envied Mae this one thing: in the evenings, as she sat quilting by hand, he would read aloud to her. Not that I wanted to quilt at night; joining a quilting circle has only made me more aware that I don't actually like to quilt. I enjoy choosing fabrics and patterns and then watching the expert quilters put them together. Oh, I push a needle through fabric, but the real pleasure on Wednesday mornings is being with and learning from these women who are near my mother's generation. (I am the only woman under seventy in the group.) Still, I thought quilting near the fireplace while a beloved voice read to me would be wonderful during long winter nights.

As Wayne's slow dying, a ten-month process, speeded up, I watched two pots of tulips I'd been given. One, an impulsive gesture from a friend, came with the buds still so tightly closed that we couldn't tell what color they'd be. I waited expectantly as the petals gradually unfolded, revealing a rich combination of blush and pale yellow. Having observed the other tulips, which arrived already open and lovely, chosen for their peachy creaminess, I know what is in store. The petals will expand, then gradually change color and drop, leaving only leaves and stem. The tulips were beautiful even in their dying. They made me think of human life, of my life: how for so long I stayed closed up tightly, not letting my colors be seen by anyone. I hope that era is ended. I want to bloom and to keep on blooming, to bring to my eventual dying a loveliness and grace.

On Wednesday mornings at Eucharist, we pray, "Help us to prepare for death with confident expectation and hope of Easter joy." Praying to make a good death seems an odd prayer to modern ears. After September 11, 2001, however, it is less strange.

Before Wayne's final illness, he drove the quilters on one of our fabric-buying *cum* lunch expeditions. As we lingered over the dessert he insisted we enjoy, he spoke of looking forward to the next great adventure: dying. A former Army Air Corps member, he regarded death not as tragedy but as the natural unfolding of the petals of life. I hope it lived up to his expectations.

Questions for Reflection

How do you respond to the passing of any beloved life?
In what ways are you preparing to make a good death?

Far from Ordinary

I like predictable. You'd think that after all the upheaval in liturgical routine that began with Advent and just culminated in Easter and Pentecost, I'd happily settle into that part of the church calendar known as Ordinary Time. Sadly, this isn't the case; although I like predictable, I also bore quickly. The fifth Sunday after Pentecost, the twelfth Sunday after Pentecost—okay, but the *twenty-seventh* Sunday after Pentecost? My eyes tire of the green vestments and begin longing for blue, purple, white again.

In ordinary time, at all times, I need a spiritual guide, someone to show me the beauty of ordinary, the necessity of quiet in a world that loves new and noisy. I do have a spiritual director, or soul friend, but she lives seventy miles away. This distance can be a good thing, especially for her; I'm less likely to call her when my demons are after me. At, say, eleven o'clock on a Monday night, I need someone nearby, and for that I have books, many of them written by women and men of faith.

May 8 is the feast day of Dame Julian of Norwich, one of my favorite medieval guides. I discovered *Revelations of Divine Love* as a first-year seminarian, a time I found spiritually and emotionally confusing. Julian lived her extraordinary life and was granted her extraordinary visions in the midst of what looked like an ordinary, routine life. How much excitement could this woman have had, not straying from two rooms attached to a church? Surely her life offered a predictable round of praying, counseling, reading, studying, and writing.

Julian's optimism and faith buoy me now in the comparative dullness of ordinary time, as they did while I was breathing the thin mountain air of seminary. Julian *believed,* despite living just down the road from the place where heretics were burned, despite three outbreaks of plague. In seminary I was certain I was losing my faith. Somehow I decided that in Julian I had found a reliable resting place. Although we were centuries apart, this medieval woman gave me courage. The reality of the communion of saints took on new meaning for me as I read Julian's words about Christ and prayer, love and longing. I took her prayer for my own, "God, of your goodness give me yourself, for you are enough for me. . . ."

Now when I reread Julian's text, I am struck by the fact of her pondering, like Mary, all that she had seen and heard. Julian recorded her visions at the time they occurred. After meditating on those visions for twenty years, she wrote a second, longer text when she was fifty, my current age. At any age, Julian reminds me, we can experience the springtime blossoming that comes after long germination. By cultivating the ordinary daily routines, out of which Julian penned her grace-filled, extraordinary words, we, too, prepare the ground of our lives for extraordinary greening.

Questions for Reflection

What events or places make up the routines of your life?
Where in these daily occurrences do you find God at work?

Trust Jesus

Several years ago, when I was regularly driving the four-hundred-mile round trip to visit my ailing mother, I was startled by navy blue block letters painted on the concrete columns supporting an overpass: Trust Jesus. Each word had been given a line of its own, the letters aligned as if the writer had all the time in the world and no fear of being discovered in the act of defacing public property.

Seeing the exhortation, I felt as though I'd received a direct word from God. In the last years of my mother's life, I was trying desperately to be more understanding and loving. It's been easy for me to forget what a chore that used to be, the way everything she did irked me as only mothers can irk their daughters. I knew that she didn't have a lot of time left and that any change had to come from me. But I dreaded the trips to Akron, and felt a mild sense of malaise when there.

Each trip, I felt my body begin tightening north of Mansfield, about an hour from my mother's home. And then as I approached Summit County, the painted words, always startling me: TRUST JESUS. They reminded me that I wasn't going into this alone, didn't have to change alone. Jesus had gone before me and would also accompany me now.

My mother has been dead nearly seven years now. I didn't get as far in loving and accepting as I had hoped, but I made some progress. Not long ago, driving in another part of Ohio, I saw the familiar encouragement again, the same printed capitals and navy blue paint: Trust Jesus. I have even seen the words on highways in other states. They're the one exception to my opposition to graffiti. I now look for them as I approach an overpass, and think about them, whether or not I see the actual blue letters.

I like to imagine some modern Johnny Appleseed sort of person out there, armed with a brush and a bucket of paint. He or she scatters seeds of hope and promise: Trust Jesus.

Questions for Reflection

In what areas of your life do you currently struggle to trust Jesus?

What reminders of past assistance might be helpful to you now?

Season of
Fullness

Spring **Summer**

Winter Autumn

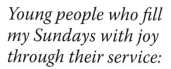

Young people who fill my Sundays with joy through their service:

Aileen	Caldwell	Ian	Lauren
Andrew	Caroline	James	Mike
Aprile	Danielle	Jenny	Sam
Ashlea	Elizabeth	Katherine	Slocomb
Brendan	Hannah	Kevin	Zoë

Painting by the Numbers

For too many years, I lived a paint-by-number life. I put blue in the sky and on the water, instead of following my heart and opting for a pink sky and dark purple water. I believed nearly every rule I was ever given; the rules offered me safety and security in a world that often seemed crazy. They told me how to live a certain kind of Christian life that would earn me the acceptance I craved. During my thirties, however, the rules stopped working. I wanted the outrageous colors of an Ohio sunset in my life, not a bland and predictable life that mimicked other lives.

And so I set off to find a new paint box. Unlike the kits I'd worked on as a child, that box didn't show me what the picture was supposed to represent or give me a chart telling me what colors to apply where. I have to admit that often my life painting looks like Jackson Pollock's art, the colors seemingly random and chance. Sometimes I stick with one huge color block for a long time, as if I were Mark Rothko. There might be heavy black lines around one image, a blurred impression, or a black-and-white photo with crisp edges. The gallery of my life keeps evolving. I don't know what style will come next, what new color I might need.

It's sometimes frightening to work without a dependable paint-by-number guide. At those times I remind myself of Saint Augustine's words, "Love God and do as you please." Augustine wasn't advocating lawlessness, but expressing his belief that one who loves God *will* do what pleases God. In the absence of a paint-by-number kit, I rely on this notion, that the desire to please God—just that—does in fact please God.

Questions for Reflection

If life is a color or palette, with what colors are you working? Do they accurately represent you?

Have you ever changed the colors you wear or the colors with which you decorate? How did that change make you feel?

Focusing on What Matters

Three Gospel writers give accounts of Jesus being transfigured on a mountain: "His face shone like the sun, and his clothes became dazzling white," Matthew 17:2 reports. Moses and Elijah, past leaders of Israel, who were well-known both as representatives of the Law and the Prophets and as two men who did not experience death, appeared to talk with Jesus. The inner circle of the apostles—Peter, James, and John—witnessed the event with astonishment. Impetuous Peter offered to build three dwellings on the spot; one for Jesus, one for Moses, and one for Elijah. Before he even finished the sentence, a voice spoke from a cloud. "This is my Son, the Beloved; with him I am well pleased; listen to him!" (Matthew 17:1–8). Don't focus on building houses while the chance to hear the words of Jesus is before you.

I experienced a similar episode of misplaced focus this week in a less dramatic setting. The acclaimed violinist Hilary Hahn came to town, and I went to hear her play Samuel Barber's *Violin Concerto.* I kept losing my way in the music, however, caught up in my admiration for Hahn's chosen outfit.

She had on a black top that sparkled at its hem; I could gaze on it without forgetting why I'd bought my ticket. But her skirt—an A-line green embroidered taffeta that swept nearly to the floor—undid me. Were those flowers or butterflies, those swirls of yellow and orange so vaguely seen from the upper balcony? Hahn herself was a butterfly, perched lightly on a stage dark with men and women wearing black.

Then I saw her shoes—little yellow strappy things, peeping out from the skirt only when she moved a certain way. They, too, sparkled. I hadn't been so fixated on shoes since the day that by happy chance I met the medieval scholar Dr. Barbara Newman, who was wearing red pumps. The choices of both women signaled that something unexpected and delightful was, quite literally, afoot.

So there I was, with every intention of hearing a virtuoso play; however, I kept defocalizing, as one of my seminary professors termed it. I'd go fuzzy, distracted by the woman who had focused most of her young life on practicing the violin and memorizing complex pieces. I wondered what it would be like to be so clear, to begin a career so young, to spend hours and hours daily in perfecting the craft.

It's not unlike the choices we each make. Where do I decide to place my focus today, this week, this year? We must all choose, or we will be swept along by the next dazzling thing that captures our eye, planning our little construction projects and missing the true music of our lives.

Questions for Reflection

In what situations do you find yourself focusing on the less important things?

How might regular meditation help you maintain focus?

Questing the Blue Heron

I am confident that I'll see the blue heron this morning, as I've seen him for the past three days. He lives in the gorge cut out by long-ago glaciers inching across Ohio, in what's called the Great Blue Hole of the Little Miami River. I round the trail's bend in anticipation—and he is not there. I look for him at each of the three places where I have, despite his camouflage, spied him out before. No.

"I sought him whom my soul loves; I sought him, but found him not," laments the Shulamite woman in the Hebrew Bible's Song of Solomon. I had begun constructing an elaborate explanation about the bird's absence, since the heron had become a Christ symbol for me. To find him involved choosing the rockiest path and going down to the depths. To find him required careful observation, so perfectly coordinated to the landscape was he. To find him meant silence. He was there to teach me stillness, standing on a rock or tiny island, balanced on one leg, moving leisurely when he walked.

Disappointed, I started back the way I had come. But then I thought I saw him, just beyond his usual spots, luring me deeper into the woods. The "heron" turned out to be a branch of a fallen tree jutting up into the air, exactly what the heron is designed to mimic. I thought of Teresa of Ávila, a reformer of the Carmelite orders during the Counter-Reformation, who wrote that as we progress in the Christian life, God often removes the spectacular signs that were once employed to draw us nearer. They are no longer needed; the honeymoon's over and we must find a way to live with Christ in the dull and daily. I thought, too, of the fourteenth-century mystic Julian of Norwich, who wrote that during her visions, she felt as if she possessed Christ and then lost him, over and over.

I didn't think that I was done learning from the beautiful heron. Nevertheless, in his absence I tried to observe what else might be along this morning's path—a pair of cardinals, a small toad, a brown bird hopping away from me, an exceptionally intricate spider web strung between trees.

I wanted the heron to be there, like magic, when I returned, but I had no real hope. That was the old, facile god, who tied things up neatly. The God I had come more recently to know was far more subtle.

Nevertheless, the heron stood on the small mud island when I returned, carelessly preening his feathers. I watched him for a few moments. Quiet and thirsty, yet satisfied as well, I moved on up the trail.

Questions for Reflection

How have you quested after God?
In what places and times have you most felt the presence of God?

Blooming Where You're Planted

A burlap wall hanging proclaiming "Bloom Where You Are Planted" was one of my needlework projects as a young adult. I was in the first years of a relatively brief but intense teaching career. I had transplanted myself from an Ohio college where I'd lived in a dorm surrounded by friends to a Florida city where I lived alone and initially knew no one. I alternated between thankfulness that I *could* make it on my own and desperate homesickness for the familiar places, climate, and people. Blooming in that foreign place, taking on a foreign role, seemed some days unlikely, if not impossible. I walked the beach, head down, collecting shells and praying for grace as I matured into my calling to teach. Sometimes I sat alone with my journal in a peaceful garden attached to an Episcopal church, watching the koi in the pool or the lizards skittering under the bougainvillea.

Regardless of the soil in which we find ourselves, God intends us to flower, and in that flowering to share our beauty with the world, to put forth the fruit of new life. In his final conversation with his followers, Jesus described the connection between them and God as that of a vine and branches. Jesus' followers were to bear fruit, as healthy fruit trees naturally do (John 15:1–16).

Walking along the Little Miami River, I'm always amazed by delicate wild violets growing out of a dead tree stump or columbine springing from the boulders along the path. There seems to be little nourishment to sustain them, and yet they bloom. Factors that I consider indispensable aren't really required; people can become the most extraordinary flowers during wars, famine, or harsh treatment. But we all need to tend this plant of our lives, to "work the earth of our hearts," as Kathleen Norris has written. Cultivating our blooms is a lifelong task, well worth the effort.

Questions for Reflection

What are the elements you need to bloom and thrive?
How are you sharing your blooming with others?

O Come Let Us Adore Him, Again

The Fourth of July has just come and gone, and at our church that means it's time to get ready for Christmas in July. Our priest, Charlotte, calls us to celebrate the Incarnation in good weather, without the usual December frenzy. We hear the Christmas readings, sing carols, and bake Christmas cookies—lots of them, so that after church, parishioners can drop off batches of them at nursing homes and at police and fire stations.

We also bring rather unusual gifts for the child, coming forward during the offering to place them at the crèche in front of the altar. Our church is situated in what has become one of the city's poorer neighborhoods. The gifts we bring are children's white T-shirts, undies, and socks. Our clergy deliver them to school principals, who distribute them to children who would not otherwise have these basics as the new school year begins.

In July we are reminded by Christ's Incarnation to value children's lives. Many of the world's poor are children. That thirty thousand of these children die every day, both of hunger and of preventable diseases, shows that we have failed to take seriously Jesus' warning that anyone who offends one of the little ones may as well hang a millstone around his neck and go swimming (Mark 9:42).

So our Christmas in July reminds me of my need to give, and give lavishly. Jesus said, "A good measure, pressed down, shaken together, running over, will be put into your lap; for the measure you give will be the measure you get back" (Luke 6:38). I "get back" at once, just by wandering department stores looking for cute socks and panties for some deserving little girl. I need our midsummer reminder of the great gift of salvation, as well as of the many blessings of my life. "What shall I return to the Lord for all his bounty to me?" Psalm 116:12 asks. A pack of kids' socks and underwear seems like a good place to begin.

Questions for Reflection

In what ways are you touching the lives of children, either your own or someone else's?

How might you incorporate something like a Christmas in July celebration in your life or your faith community?

Summer Abundance

One evening while I was walking to the library, two tiny blond girls cried out to me from their front porch. The wind carried away all but their last two words, "for sale."

"*What* is for sale?" I asked, seeing no lemonade pitcher or toys being recycled.

"Nature for sale!" they repeated in a singsong duo, and sure enough, each child had a cache of stones and twigs piled next to her. I wanted to tell them that you can't sell nature; it's free, like all of God's graces. Instead, I lamented to them that I was sorry, but I had no money with me. They insisted that I didn't need any money; I could just take something.

Perhaps you can't sell nature, but most Saturdays from early spring until late fall, I walk to the farmer's market. The rows of stalls heaped with produce, jams, herbs, flowers, soaps, and honey remind me of God's abundance and generosity. "The hills gird themselves with joy," Psalm 65 states, "The valleys deck themselves with grain," and so they do. I also garner this sense of abundance by driving along miles of cornfields—especially when the corn fences from my sight everything that is not tall and green and rustling.

After receiving a windfall—lovely image, that, of fruit just lying on the ground requiring no effort to gather—from my writing recently, I wanted to make a symbolic purchase. A piece of jewelry, I thought. When it was admired, I'd tell about the miracle of being a working writer, of God's grace in giving me the desires of my heart, as Psalm 37 promises.

However, instead I impulsively bought an old redwood wardrobe to which someone had added shelves: a perfect pantry. My friend Joe helped me get the cabinet home, and I hauled out all the foodstuffs from the cramped kitchen cabinet and placed them lovingly on those shelves. It serves as a visible reminder of God's abundant provision.

It also prompts me to remember other pantries—the one at my church, for example, which distributes food every Wednesday afternoon—and other opportunities to give. I need not hoard like the squirrels skittering in the woods, a morsel for winter tightly grasped in their jaws. From my pantry ingredients this week, I will bake cookies for a prison ministry, sending of my abundance to men whose lives hold less sweetness than my own. And in return I will know an increase of spirit for sharing what I have so richly been given.

Questions for Reflection

What visible symbols do you associate with God's generosity? With what outreach ministries are you involved or could you become involved?

Follow Me

The stories of two good men, separated by nineteen centuries, have been on my mind recently.

In the church in which I grew up, children weren't allowed to worship with the adults until we were in junior high and presumably knew how to behave. To that end, during sixth grade we were permitted to join the adults on the first Sunday of the month, learning to participate in a Communion service. This was a Baptist church; once a month we'd pass one another silver plates covered with cracker bits and silver trays of grape juice in small but heavy individual glasses.

I was then the only one in my family who went to church, taken there by kind neighbors. I made an alternative family of my peers, whose religious families intrigued me. Cynthia, for example, was the only child of her parents, Richard and Helen, who coordinated their wardrobes for Sunday. (For a long time, I regarded the chance to wear matching blazers as a premier reason for marriage.) Helen, an accountant, was the church treasurer. Cynthia sang in the choir and played violin solos.

Week after week Richard sat next to his wife, upright and handsome, tears in his eyes whenever Cynthia performed. He made no claim to believe and never reached for a cracker or glass of juice as he passed the trays.

Richard, the present but left-out father, strikes me as a modern example of Zebedee, the father of James and John. Matthew reports that Jesus called Zebedee's sons after a night of fishing, while they were mending their nets. They left their father and the boats and nets that were their livelihood. Their mother, Salome, also followed Jesus and supported him. Zebedee continued fishing, though I wonder how he managed. Peter and Andrew, whom Jesus also called, were partners with James and John and Zebedee. The older man lost four strong, young workers; surely he'd hoped to pass on the business to his sons. What were the days like for him, when James and John tramped with Jesus and other men—women following, too—while he hauled in fish and mended the nets alone? Did "the boys" come home and recount the miracles they had seen? Did Jesus ever show up for a meal, as he did at Peter's, and did he and Zebedee then sit down and talk? Did Zebedee believe in his own way, sticking to what he knew and providing for his family and, indirectly, for Jesus?

We don't know, just as James and John didn't know all that would be asked of them. None of us knows. But when we hear our names called, we get up and follow. Our parents, our friends, our business associates may never understand or embrace what we are called to do. But the best of them, like Richard and Zebedee, show up for us anyway, dependable and proud.

Questions for Reflection

Who has served for you as a model of reliability?
How are you demonstrating steadfastness to others?

Letting Go of the Sky

I've finished the work due next Monday, and am taking the weekend off. There are four possibilities on my radar screen—good, wholesome, interesting options. I'm choosing none of them, even though two are right here. I could have an "I'm not leaving the village" day; instead I've decided on a "I'm going no farther than the mailbox" day.

Periodically I need such days. To an outsider, they might not look much different than my working days. I still read and write in my favorite recliner. I still stare at the computer screen, pet the cats, and nibble my way through the day. I might even tackle a load of laundry or dishes. Despite the surface similarities, however, today is still a day off; I'm not trying to achieve anything.

My friends may well laugh at my distinctions, because I am a Type-B personality and in no apparent danger of working myself to death. I don't rush and I don't much worry about things that don't get done. After years of experience, I've learned that the plates and cups will still be in the sink when I get around to them.

Some months ago, while rummaging in my friend Bobbi's collage box, I found a great still life painted in bold colors. On the back of the painting was a bonus, a poem called "Letting Go of the Sky." The poet speaks of holding up a corner of the sky, of being deemed keeper of the sky, by both herself and those who depend on her.

Like most people I know, I've staked out my corner of the

sky. Will it really fall if I take some time off to be utterly unproductive? After all, even Jesus, who had a great mission to complete in a short time, invited his disciples to "come away to a deserted place all by yourselves and rest a while" after their return from a preaching tour (Mark 6:31). Once in a while, it's good to give yourself the luxury of an unstructured, slow day, a day to bore yourself. Like the dishes in my sink, we'll all be here when you get back.

Questions for Reflection

When was the last time you allowed yourself a day—or an hour—to do nothing?

What keeps you from doing so, and how might you change that?

Let It Shine

In Matthew, chapter 5, Jesus tells his followers that they are the light of the world. No one would light a lamp and then cover it with a bushel basket, he said. That seems obvious enough. Jesus explains that they are to let their lights shine, not for their own glory, but so that others will see and glorify God for the gifts they've received and put to good use.

I thought of that passage tonight at the library, where I saw a fine actor who lives in our village. I wanted to tell him how much I appreciated his work, especially his last show. But my mind turned eggbeater on me. I couldn't remember what that last show had been, or what he'd done so marvelously. I didn't want to sound like an agent: "Love your work. Have your people call my people." So I backed away and stared at DVD titles for a while. By the time I remembered the name of the show, and what about his performance had most deeply touched me, both he and the opportunity were gone.

This wasn't only about my brain going all gelatin-y in the presence of someone I admire. It was also about not wanting to appear a fool by stuttering or becoming speechless.

So I offer this to the many people I admire, the many people I will never be able to meet or in whose company I will become tongue-tied:

Thank you for the years of work you've spent honing your craft, whether it's woodworking, playing the xylophone, spinning the potter's wheel, caring for others, or repairing computers.

Thanks for investing huge chunks of your life to make what you do look elegant and effortless, bringing joy to others by exercising your gifts. Your work encourages me to take my own light from under the bushel basket and let it shine.

Questions for Reflection

Who are some of the people whose work you most admire?
    Why?
How can you tell them?

Asking the Right Questions

"Why do you always have to ask the hard questions?" a frustrated friend flattered me by asking shortly before I left for seminary. I had no good answer for him; hard questions seemed to me as unavoidable as the spring rains. Part of my reason for attending seminary was to get some answers to those questions. Not that it worked out that way, of course—I left with even more questions than I'd brought and a deepened knowledge that answers aren't easy to come by.

Lunching and talking deeply with a friend today, I remembered some of the questions that have shaped the second half of my life. During my thirties I read a book by Miriam Adeney, *Time for Risking: Priorities for Women.* She posed the question, "What kind of old woman do you want to be?" I have no memory of her own answer, but that question started me thinking about the way that days accumulate into old age. I wouldn't suddenly cross some magical threshold and become someone I hadn't been, as I used to hope I would at twenty-five or forty. Thus, I had to begin consciously building into my life the qualities I wanted to manifest at seventy.

The second question came from Elizabeth Canham's book *Heart Whispers,* which I read after seminary. "What kind of life does my heart want?" Having no obvious link from seminary training to career, I had by grace stumbled into work as an editor. However, I was still circling around the one thing my heart had always wanted: to write. For more than two decades, I had supported myself first by teaching about writing and books, and then, when I worked in a library, by helping students find answers in the writings of others. Still later, I began editing the words other people wrote. It was time, I decided, to stop standing with my nose pressed against the glass of the candy counter and to get on with the life *I* wanted, the life of a writer.

Now five years into life as a full-time writer, I am in a continual state of amazement. In the Sermon on the Mount, Jesus said, "Ask, and it will be given you; search, and you will find; knock, and the door will be opened for you" (Matthew 7:7). If we keep on asking the right questions and being honest in our answers, the rest will be given to us.

Questions for Reflection

*How would you spend your life if practical concerns were not
an issue?*
*What small steps can you take in the direction of that
dream?*

Slow Flowering

Pink, yellow, green, lilac, and blue petals cover my desk. No, not flower petals, but those that have fluttered from the various Post-it packs that serve as a prime color accent in my home. Indeed, commenting on my great reliance on these nifty little squares, a friend once suggested that my brain was nothing but Post-it notes. I keep stacks of them everywhere I might want to jot down an idea for an essay, a call to make, or what to fix for supper.

Yet they began as a mistake, these mildly sticky little friends. In trying to invent a strong adhesive, a 3M scientist instead made a weaker one. No one knew what to do with it; for four years it sat around the lab. One Sunday morning another 3M scientist, who was also a church choir member, became frustrated at his attempts to keep his markers in the right hymns. Remembering his colleague's weak glue, he coated his hymnal markers with it, and realized the potential of this former flop. In 1980, ten years after the weak adhesive had been invented, Post-it Notes finally came on the market.

This accidental invention serves as a cautionary tale for me. I am often too quick to judge—and judge harshly—what I have created, whether it's a piece of writing or a life decision that isn't working out the way I'd planned. Actions and ideas have consequences, and they don't always play out in the time span suggested by half-hour sit-coms or two-hour movies of the week. By contrast, God seems to take the long view; Jesus lived thirty years of what looked like a normal Jewish male's life before his final three years of public ministry. The apparent train wreck that was the last week of his life led to resurrection and hope for multitudes over thousands of years.

I've come to believe that God doesn't waste anything. The classes I took that didn't interest me, the time I invested in friendships that died, the apparently unnoticed acts of kindness: let's not be too quick to judge what we consider our mistakes, to toss out new ideas that don't seem useful quite yet. Flowers, inventions, and life goals don't always bloom overnight.

Questions for Reflection

What in your life are you nearly ready to give up on?
What steps can you take to preserve that thing and wait for
its time to come?

The Sweets of Scripture

To avoid the real possibility of teacher burnout and to keep the kids themselves from being bored, this year three of us have rotated the task of teaching the teenagers in my church. I've done my two segments already and am finished for the year. It's a relief not needing to prepare a lesson, even though that preparation is good for me. Here's the truth: I miss teaching Sunday school.

One of the components I've missed lately is my Saturday evening baking ritual. When I began teaching, I determined to bake treats from scratch and with love and to serve them for our snacks. The idea was hardly original. In the stage version of *Crossing Delancey,* Sam says he likes to attend the Jewish morning worship before heading to work, to get "a taste of something sweet in the mouth." The *sweet* of course is the Scripture; Psalm 119:103 proclaims, "How sweet are your words to my taste, sweeter than honey to my mouth!" The prophet Jeremiah picks up the theme, writing, "Your words were found, and I ate them, and your words became to me a joy and the delight of my heart" (15:16).

That's what I want for the teenagers in Sunday school, and for all of us: to know the sweetness of Scripture study.

My weekly baking required nearly as much preparation as the lessons themselves. Basic supplies had to be kept on hand and organized. Clean dishes and some clear counter space were required to mix a batch of cookies and set them to cool. There had to be dedicated time.

I miss the rhythm of it. I miss having leftover cookies in the freezer to serve anyone who might drop by during the week or to take to quilting. Because I am woefully undisciplined when I don't have a project at hand, I miss the regular study of Scripture on a deep level.

The sweetness of the cookies, the sweetness of Scripture, the sweetness of the young lives gathered each week: confection for the soul!

Questions for Reflection

What have you found to be sweet about the study of Scripture? What regular rhythms and rituals do you follow to enjoy time with God?

The Last Word

The date on my first rejection letter for the first book I submitted to a real New York publisher is August 6, 1963. I was twelve, gentle reader, and I wanted, like Jo March in *Little Women*, to be a writer. I'd already written thirteen books, and so I sent to Abelard-Schuman in New York what I considered my best, *The Mystery at Lazy C Ranch*, its sixty-page handwritten manuscript held together with staples and a construction paper cover. That work was most kindly rejected; with the undaunted spirit of a true writer, I persevered. The following year my best friend created a watercolor book cover for one of my new manuscripts. We were going to be a famous duo, he the artist and I the writer.

By the end of high school, I'd received rejections for my poetry as well. I went to college, got a teaching job, submitted an article to be rejected now and then, but mostly went quiet. I wrote regularly, just stopped sending out anything. I "lost" twenty years doing that. I might still be writing and putting the results in boxes under the bed if I hadn't joined a writing group.

The writer of Proverbs says that "the desire accomplished is sweet to the soul" (13:19). You are holding my first published book in your hands, an accomplished desire that has been more than four decades in coming. A few poems and articles have been published; one essay was even anthologized. But this is the first book.

I tell Caldwell, one of the talented teens at my church,

Don't go quiet. Don't just practice the piano and write your compositions and never let them be heard. Keep at it. Develop a thick hide. Write it down, play it, send it out. We are all meant to sing out our *selves,* Victorian poet Gerard Manley Hopkins writes in his sonnet, "As kingfishers catch fire." *What I do is me: for that I came.* Sing out your self in whatever way is you: paint, teach, draw, act, dance, sing, design clothing, write, sculpt, leap, sew, cook, throw pots, garden, raise children. You have a unique contribution to offer us, and we are the poorer if you hug it to yourself for fear it will get bruised out there. We are all of us, by the grace of God, more robust than we know.

Questions for Reflection

In what ways do you "sing out" your self?
What steps can you take to do so more boldly?

Acknowledgments

No writer has ever been blessed with a more supportive group of friends and colleagues. Elizabeth Visick advertised for a writing group more than a decade ago. In this, as in so much else, she has no idea of her gifts to me. That group offered me a place to hear my own voice and to grow as a writer. Special thanks to Kristina Manuel Onder, Liz Porter, and MaryJo Werthman White for many years of writing, reading, editing, laughing, and eating together.

Mary Beth Pringle, ideal reader and coach, has honed my words and thinking over several years. Her continual support and understanding of what I'm trying to do is a boon. I am grateful to Gary Wayne Barker, Bobbi Gill, and Joseph Messner, who also read sections of this manuscript, for their comments and ongoing friendship. Adrianne Oliss gave this work her usual elegant editing and saved me from embarrassing errors.

Without Margaret Fenton, this book wouldn't have happened. Margaret and I met in seminary; her job has always been to challenge me to grow. She suggested that I contact Amanda Stone Cushing, the program director for Columbus, Ohio's Spirituality Network. Amanda, who has the dubious honor of always thinking I have good ideas, offered me a forum for leading workshops and publishing my meditations; some in this book have appeared in earlier forms in the *Spirituality Network Newsletter.* I am likewise grateful for all those, especially Margaret Leis Hanna, who have attended the Network-sponsored workshops.

I have been blessed by the people of Christ Episcopal Church in Springfield, Ohio. The Reverend Charlotte Collins Reed has encouraged my writing for the Church and given me much, through both her sermons and her years of friendship. In addition, the persistent faith and friendship of the Reverend Kathi Kramer, who inveigled me into teaching Sunday school, has brought me a great and unexpected joy.

Profoundest gratitude goes to the community of faith at the Methodist Theological School in Ohio, which gave me a strong branch on which to hang my chrysalis during my faith metamorphosis. Special mention must be made of my professors in Bible and in Church History: Paul Wesley Chilcote (now teaching at Duke Divinity School), C. M. Kempton Hewitt, Jeffrey Jaynes, Diane L. Lobody, and Frederick C. Tiffany. Their teaching nourishes me still.

Other friends deserving thanks for their ongoing support include Sharon Bidwell, Katherine Bundy, Jan and Jerry Elve, Ellen Fox, Lori Greenawalt, Deborah Bush Haffey, Eric Helmuth, Patricia Henrich, Sharon Luster, Diane and Mahlon Merchant, and Larry and Margaret Strawn. My brother, John Edward Johnson, and his family have made my life possible.

For their examples and their writing, I am indebted to Sue Bender, Roberta Bondi, Barbara Crafton, Annie Dillard, Anne Lamott, Madeleine L'Engle, Nancy Mairs, and Kathleen Norris. Attending writing workshops with Patricia Hampl, Haven Kimmel, Lynne Sharon Schwartz, and Sue Monk Kidd has offered grace upon grace.

Deep appreciation goes to Ulrike Guthrie, whose skill in both concision and poetry has greatly improved these pages. Without the encouragement of Michael Wilt of Cowley Publications, this book could not have come into being. For his willingness to take a risk on a new writer, I am ever grateful.